"*Experiential Worship* shows not only why thinking beyond preaching and singing is biblical but also how to begin worshiping with our heart, mind, soul, and body."

DAN KIMBALL, author of *The Emerging Church*

"Bob Rognlien takes us beyond black-and-white text orientation, metaphorical exploration, and mere worship construction to a place where heart, soul, mind, and strength can connect with God in experience."

HANDT HANSON
director of worship arts, Prince of Peace, Burnsville, Minnesota

"Bob Rognlien has made a significant contribution to the dialogue surrounding how all of us who are entrusted to facilitate worship can do our job with greater biblical, historical, and cultural understanding."

NANCY BEACH
arts director, Willow Ministries
Willow Creek Community Church, South Barrington, Illinois

"Bob Rognlien has moved from theory to strategy and then practice. This is a road map for developing effective worship that no longer talks about God but ushers the believer into the very presence of God. Pastors and worship leaders need to read this book—and then do it!"

REVEREND DR. MICHAEL W. FOSS
senior pastor, Prince of Peace, Burnsville, Minnesota

"Bob Rognlien's loving but incisive work shatters the long-held mythology that information is key to transformation, and it does so with great care. Rognlien's worship practice and theology is the result of solid study and a life of humble experience."

SALLY MORGENTHALER
worship innovator; author of *Worship Evangelism*

ENCOUNTERING GOD
WITH HEART, SOUL, MIND,
AND STRENGTH

Experiential
WORSHIP

Bob Rognlien

NAVPRESS®

The Navigators is an international Christian organization. Our mission is to advance the gospel of Jesus and His kingdom into the nations through spiritual generations of laborers living and discipling among the lost. We see a vital movement of the gospel, fueled by prevailing prayer, flowing freely through relational networks and out into the nations where workers for the kingdom are next door to everywhere.

NavPress is the publishing ministry of The Navigators. The mission of NavPress is to reach, disciple, and equip people to know Christ and make Him known by publishing life-related materials that are biblically rooted and culturally relevant. Our vision is to stimulate spiritual transformation through every product we publish..

ISBN-13: 978-1-57683-663-7
ISBN-10: 1-57683-663-0

Cover design by David Uttley, UDG / DesignWorks, Inc.
Cover image by Corbis
Creative Team: Rachelle Gardner, Arvid Wallen, Cara Iverson, Glynese Northam

Some of the anecdotal illustrations in this book are true to life and are included with the permission of the persons involved. All other illustrations are composites of real situations, and any resemblance to people living or dead is coincidental.

Unless otherwise identified, all Scripture quotations in this publication are taken from the *New Revised Standard Version* (NRSV), copyright © 1989, by the Division of Christian Education of the National Council of the Churches of Christ in the USA, used by permission, all rights reserved.

Rognlien, Bob, 1964-
   Experiential worship : encountering God with heart, soul, mind, and strength / Bob Rognlien.
      p. cm.
   "Bringing truth to life."
   Includes bibliographical references (p.   ).
   ISBN 1-57683-663-0
   1. Public worship. I. Title.
   BV15.R64 2005
   264--dc22

                                        2004019509

Printed in the United States of America

4 5 6 7 8 9 10 / 12 11 10 09 08

To Pam, Bobby, and Luke,
the joy and crown of my life;
and to the people of Good Shepherd,
faithful partners on this divine adventure
of loving God with heart, soul, mind, and strength.

For what is our hope or joy or crown of boasting
before our Lord Jesus at his coming?
Is it not you?
Yes, you are our glory and joy!
1 THESSALONIANS 2:19-20

"Western Christianity went to sleep in a modern world governed by the gods of reason and observation. It is awakening in a post-modern world open to revelation and hungry for experience. . . . It is one thing to talk about God. It is quite another thing to experience God."

LEONARD SWEET, POST-MODERN PILGRIMS

CONTENTS

PART FIVE—HEARTWORSHIP:
ENGAGING AND TRANSFORMING THE WILL

PART SIX—MAKING IT HAPPEN!
A PATHWAY FOR IMPLEMENTING EXPERIENTIAL WORSHIP

FOREWORD

My Swedish grandfather had a saying: "You don't know a man until you've had dealings with him." In other words, you've got to see a person in action if you're going to know his real character. How does he behave when he's in the winner's circle? What does he do when the going gets rough? Does he spend most of his time pontificating and ordering people around, or is he mild-mannered and patient, preferring to work behind the scenes? Does he walk into a room with a swagger, expecting everyone to turn his way, or does he sit down and wait his turn to be noticed? Does his handshake communicate confidence, control, or compassion? All of these experiences comprise the data we use every day to evaluate a person's true nature and determine what relationship we'd like (or not like) to have with him.

Grandpa Bennett practiced the motto he preached. He never closed a large deal with another farmer without testing him out on a small deal first. If the farmer passed that test, Grandpa then proposed the big deal. He'd walk his future partner out to the back forty to "chew the fat" out of range of prying ears. Then they'd both sit down to a big farm spread and finally seal their agreement with a mug of homemade brew.

Knowing someone means collecting "data" from every source possible: conversation, behavior, vocal inflection, body language, even the messages encoded in a touch. It's interesting to note that most of this data can't be collected via the left brain. Grandpa Bennett didn't rely on dossiers and fact sheets when he picked a partner. Certainly, it was helpful to know what his neighbor's wheat crop had done last year and whether he was up to date on his tractor payments. But Grandpa needed more than this. He needed to see—to experience—what made this guy tick.

If that is true on a human level, how much more true it is of our relationship with God. We don't really know God until we've had dealings with him. God's dossier and fact sheets are voluminous, and they're crucial to our complete understanding of who God is. Yet to truly know God, we must press past the God-data—beyond our theologies, creeds, bullet points, sermon notes, and vision statements—to real-time encounters. Just as my grandfather's dealings with people involved all of his senses (watching for visual cues, listening to vocal inflection, interpreting the handshake or pat on the back, enjoying a meal together, and enacting rural rituals), our dealings with God require no less.

It is significant that we even need to have a book titled *Experiential Worship*. Bob Rognlien's passionate offering in this book is nothing less than a reality check. It is a de facto admission that the word *worship* no longer means what it did in ancient times: a multisensory engagement with the God of the universe. Somewhere along the way, we abandoned the rich, Judeo foundation of sign, symbol, ritual, incense, and movement. We discarded the multifaceted gatherings of the early Christians: sacrament as splendid feasts, mind-sharpening odes to the triune God, unedited psalmody (we forget how familiar the early Christians were with grief), exuberant, spontaneous thanksgiving, and vibrant narrative.

It has been said that Protestantism is the spirituality of print. Is this an exaggerated statement? Certainly. Even Martin Luther, the father of the Reformation, viewed worship as whole-person response. He may have dubbed worship "the school of the church," yet Luther's school included symbol, image, music, ritual, sacrament, mystery, and a clear, theological bent away from modern self-determinism. Still, enlightenment Protestantism did not escape the lure of rationalism, and consequently the "spirituality of print" epithet does speak some truth. For far too long, we have imagined that information was the key to transformation, that if one only had enough God-data in the cerebral cortex, one would have God. Bob Rognlien—pastor, worship leader, and craftsman—knows better. His loving but incisive work shatters this long-held mythology and does so with great care. Rognlien's worship theology is the result of solid study, his worship practice honed by years of experience, his personal worship life a rich and humble journey, and his worship passion unmistakable—to engage people with God with every sense and at every possible level.

There is much talk these days of worship for twentysomethings—services crafted specifically for emerging generations. If Bob had wanted to jump on the GenX bandwagon, he could have titled this book *Emerging Experiences: Worship for Postmoderns*. But he didn't, and I, for one, am glad. You see, Bob realizes what is really happening. It is not only twentysomethings who have moved beyond the frontal lobe to encounter God; it is all of us. It is the fortysomething single dad, shattered and left for dead on the side of the marital road—he's way past bullet points and outlines. It is the eightysomething grandmother, her arthritic hands painting an Advent mural with her twentysomething granddaughter—she's way past liturgy-on-cruise-control. And it's thirteen-year-old Jessica at the controls of the LCD projector, showing a video version she and her friends created of the Apostles' Creed. Ironically, Jessica and her friends are already beyond emerging worship—the creation of some cool, hi-tech enclave just for high-school kids. They'd rather be involved with the gray-hairs—those on the back side of forty-five. Their only requirement is to be viewed as equals in the worship-crafting process and to be able to create a little mess now and then.

If we want to talk about what is emerging, let's talk about this: the human family, hungering en masse to bring their real selves—their unedited, whole selves—to a real God. Whether your congregation is seventysomething or twentysomething, give them the gift of complete access. Give them worship as a whole-person, no-holds-barred experience—an unforgettable "dealing" with the God who is here and waiting.

SALLY MORGENTHALER
FOUNDER, SACRAMENTIS.COM AND DIGITAL GLASS PRODUCTIONS

ACKNOWLEDGMENTS

Whatever good has come from my life is largely a result of God's grace flowing to me through people. This book is no exception. I am forever indebted to all those who have supported, shaped, and inspired me to write about worshiping God with heart, soul, mind, and strength: my cousin and inspiration Lisa Tawn Bergren, who first helped me believe I could write; my dear friend Rachelle Gardner, who shared my dream, showed me how to make it a reality, and then became my editor to make this a far better book; my brothers in the ministry, who have given me faithful support and accountability in pastors' groups through the years; Sally Morgenthaler, who has generously been my mentor, teacher, and guide; Robert Webber, who showed me that the future does in fact run through the past; Richard Foster, who opened my eyes to the historical streams of worship traditions; Dana Hanson, Ryan Warne-McGraw, and Chris Taylor, who kindly read the manuscript and gave invaluable insights; and the amazing staff, leaders, and members of Good Shepherd, who have joined me on this adventure of Experiential Worship and provided me with a sabbatical to put it into words, particularly Ray Schnurr, who first challenged me to come out of my box; Christy Saville, who put hands and feet to my visions; Greg Wallace, the best pastoral partner I could hope for; and Mark and Lea Emerson, who set my ministry to beautiful music. Beyond anything having to do with this book, I thank the members of my entire family, who have patiently cheered me on and always believed in me, especially the crown of my life—Pam, Bobby, and Luke—you are my greatest joy. Above all, I give thanks and praise to the One who alone is worthy of all my heart, soul, mind, and strength: Jesus Christ. To him be all glory, honor, and praise!

Introduction

WORSHIP FOR THE WHOLE PERSON

You shall love the Lord your God with all your heart, and with all your soul,
and with all your mind, and with all your strength.

MARK 12:30

A HEART STORY

I stuck out like a sore white thumb, but no one else seemed to notice or care. I was definitely underdressed; every woman there wore a hat and dress, every man a suit and tie. I was mesmerized by the choir; their deep soulful voices enveloped me with the most luxuriant gospel music I had ever heard.

As the pastor climbed up into the huge mahogany pulpit, he quickly took hold of the entire congregation. "Look at me now!" he ordered, and all present gave him their full attention. He proceeded to recount the parable of the prodigal son in a way that made me a participant in the story. Each line was echoed in choruses of "Amen!" "Preach," and "Go on!" from the pews.

The pastor described how the father in the story stood on the porch, scanning the horizon for his lost son. Now he began to conclude by imploring us in his deep, booming voice, "Can you see the Father standing on the porch, calling to your heart, 'Come home, my child, come home!'?"

The music began and the pastor stepped down from the pulpit saying, "If you have wandered far and squandered much, today the Father invites you to come home. Come and trade your rags for riches, your guilt for glory. Come now and never look back!" As we began to sing, people started trickling one by one down the aisles, and lay ministers came forward to pray with them. I didn't go forward, but in my heart I wanted to come home. Deep within I resolved to stop squandering my spiritual inheritance, and I took a deliberate step toward my heavenly Father.

A SOUL STORY

I felt a twinge of apprehension as the music started. The air was electric with the sense that anything could happen in this church. Soon the people were on their feet, swaying to the rhythm. I found myself standing and clapping, swept along by the rising tide of praise to God. I had never sung these songs before, but that didn't seem to matter.

The words weren't as important as the energy building in the room. At one point, I realized the people around me were no longer singing with intelligible words at all. Somehow the most amazing blend of sounds was dancing with the music, and I felt a shiver run down my spine. Deep in my soul, I began to express love and awe and wonder to the God who created me and loved me far beyond words.

I don't remember much about the subject of the sermon or exactly what the preacher said. What stands out was the emotion that came through every syllable. Mopping sweat from his brow with a towel, he finally took off his jacket so nothing would stand in the way of his passionate message that God's love has the power to heal us here and now.

When he finished preaching, the singing resumed and we were back on our feet, swaying and clapping to the music. I'm not sure when it started, but suddenly I realized tears were streaming down my cheeks. It felt good, like a cleansing release of hidden pain. Driving home, I couldn't explain all that had happened, but I knew I had encountered God and that his love had touched my soul.

A MIND STORY

The academic robe only added to the professorial air of the minister as she spoke. Clearly this was someone who was steeped in biblical studies and educated as a scholar of the faith. But this was no abstract intellectual lecture;

it was a teaching so clear and deep it quenched the thirsty questions that flooded my mind.

The complex theology of Paul became simple and yet more profound as we delved ever deeper into the reading from Romans assigned for that day. Every sentence contained another gem of insight into the meaning of grace and faith and salvation. What had always been an obtuse passage to me now seemed a bottomless treasure chest as the preacher mined its truth to set us free.

When we stood to sing the sermon hymn, I realized it had been carefully chosen to reiterate the message. As I sang the verses, the truths we had just heard began to take root in my mind. Proclaiming the ancient creed, I saw more clearly how these gems fit into the timeless truth of the age-old Christian faith.

For the first time, I began to truly understand how the paradox of God's perfect holiness and his endless mercy embrace in the scandal of Christ crucified. This wasn't just an abstract idea that fascinated me but a gripping realization that took hold of my consciousness and unlocked another door in the prison of my ignorance. Walking out of the church, my mind was reeling with thoughts and questions, and I knew I would never see the cross in the same way again.

A Strength Story

The colored light of stained-glass windows washed over my weary body like a soothing breeze on a hot summer's day. At first I couldn't place the smell but then realized the strange odor tickling my nose was incense rising up from the altar. Settling into a wooden pew, the deep notes of a massive pipe organ reverberated off ancient stone vaults overhead and penetrated my bones. I resonated with the mystery of how huge yet close God really is.

The liturgy was complicated and hard to follow, but countless biblical allusions wove a rich tapestry of praise and worship to God. The priest seemed to be doing much of the work with intricate rituals, chants, and readings, but the people were fully engaged—sitting, kneeling, crossing themselves, standing, and sitting again. The priest's chants were followed by responses from the congregation—a sacred dialogue, like good friends sharing important thoughts over a meal.

During one of the readings, I noticed a painting that depicted the very scene we were hearing in the words of Scripture. The artwork on the walls reminded me that we are indeed surrounded by "so great a cloud of witnesses" (Hebrews 12:1). As the priest consecrated the elements for Communion, I looked beyond the raised chalice of wine into the carved face of Jesus on the cross above and heard the familiar words in a completely new way: "This cup that is poured out for you is the new covenant in my blood" (Luke 22:20).

As the service came to a close, we stood to receive the ancient Aaronic blessing, and I pictured that Hebrew priest of old speaking those same words over the gathered people of Israel. It was as if time was compressed and all of God's people from every time and place were gathered together in one mystical communion under the blessing of Christ. Though it wasn't my normal practice, I even tried crossing myself as the priest concluded, "In the name of the Father, and the Son, and the Holy Spirit, amen." Drawing in a deep breath, I felt peace and new strength flooding my body, and I knew God had literally touched me that day.

THE STORY BEYOND THE STORIES

Four different churches. Four unique encounters with God. Four distinct pieces in the mosaic of my worship experience. How have *you* encountered God in corporate worship? Is your experience of God more emotional or more intellectual? Does worship primarily engage your physical senses, or does it inspire you to make concrete decisions? All of us who feel strongly about worship have encountered God in ways that have shaped our lives and formed our convictions of what worship services "should" be like.

Maybe your experience of God has called you to very clear and specific commitments. Perhaps you can cite the actual day and moment you gave your life to Christ. Many worship services you have attended seem wishy-washy, never closing the deal, never calling people to actually live their faith. For you, worship should lead people to make concrete decisions and take specific steps as followers of Jesus. This experience reflects the *volitional* aspect of worship that has been captured by the Baptist, Methodist, Holiness, and Evangelical traditions. In movements such as the Great Awakening and in such people as John Wesley and Billy Graham, we can see how God has stirred up the hearts of his people and changed their lives through worship experiences that empower a response of the will.

Or perhaps you have had profoundly moving experiences of God's saving power in your life. Many worship services you have attended seem dead, as if the participants are going through the motions without any real spiritual power. You identify with worship that is emotive, dynamic, and openly expressive. This experience comprises the *emotional* aspect of worship that has been captured so well by the Revivalist, Pentecostal, and Charismatic traditions. Whether it was in the so-called "burned-over district," Revivalist tent meetings, or the phenomenon at the Azusa Street Mission, we can see how God has moved in history to stir up the souls of his people and change their lives through intense emotional experiences of worship.

Or you might have experienced God primarily through a cognitive understanding of the truth. Many worship services you have attended seem shallow and superficial, offering trite clichés and manufactured emotions in place of the truth. You understand worship as a learning process in which people come to comprehend more and more of who God is as revealed to us in the Bible. This experience conveys the *intellectual* experience of worship that is exemplified through the Lutheran, Reformed (Presbyterian), and Bible Church traditions. In the time of the Reformation, through such people as Martin Luther and John Calvin, we can see how God has lifted up his Word and transformed the minds of his people with an intellectual experience of worship.

Or possibly you have experienced God in mysterious and wonderful ways through concrete, tangible expressions of worship, such as ritual and sacrament. Many worship services you have attended seem bland and one-dimensional, with people talking about God but never actually engaging him directly. For you, worship is a sensory experience, in which God is encountered through physical expressions of his glory, majesty, and love. This experience embodies the *physical* aspect of worship that has best been captured by the Orthodox, Roman Catholic, and Anglican (Episcopal) traditions. In patriarchs such as Augustine and John Chrysostom, in saints such as Francis of Assisi and Mother Teresa, through liturgy and art that date back to the early centuries of Christianity, we can see how God has strengthened the church and changed lives through powerful physical experiences of worship.

Each of the stories above represents a different aspect of human experience in worship that has been championed by various movements in the history of the church.

HISTORICAL WORSHIP EMPHASES

HISTORICAL MOVEMENTS	ASPECT EMPHASIZED	INTENDED RESULT
Orthodox/Catholic/Anglican	Physical	Specific actions
Lutheran/Reformed/ Bible Church	Intellectual	Clear understanding
Methodist/Baptist/Evangelical	Volitional	Concrete decisions
Pentecostal/Charismatic	Emotional	Powerful feelings

All Christians have a view of corporate worship that is shaped by personality, experience, and these historical emphases. Our presuppositions about the way worship "should be" are largely the results of how we have experienced God in the past. The beauty of this is that God works uniquely in the life of every person on the planet—we each have our own story with God! And in the broader sense, each worship tradition has its own story, its own function in the history of Christianity. However, the tragedy of these presuppositions is that they lead us to institutionalize and systematize that particular aspect of the worship experience. We determine that this is the way worship is "supposed to be," and we ignore or reject other approaches. Even if this is not openly expressed, we all have our quiet bias and subtle pride that not only devalues other traditions but also keeps us from experiencing the full power of holistic biblical worship. When we start to see the bigger picture of biblical worship across traditions and throughout history, we take a step toward the rediscovery of what I call "Experiential Worship."

DISCOVERING THE GRAND STORY

Admittedly, I am painting a picture with broad strokes and historical generalizations. Space prohibits including all of the variations of Christian worship, such as Mennonites and Quakers, Congregationalists and Camp-bellites, to name a few. But if we look closely, we can place our own tribe within these categories of worship experience: emotional, volitional, intellectual, and physical.

Of course, no tradition is defined by only one aspect of human experience, but each tends to emphasize one over the others. Usually, we can also identify a secondary strength within a tradition. For instance, Baptists emphasize the will with their altar calls but also address the intellect through their biblical teaching. Lutherans, with their theology of the Word, are strong on intellect but also involve the physical through the sacraments. The Orthodox church offers a profoundly physical worship experience yet clearly calls people to obedience with specific acts of the will. Pentecostal churches focus on emotions but also invite people into a very physical expression of worship.

Each tradition has captured only a portion of the full range of biblical worship, constricting its inherent life-changing power. We will experience God in transforming ways as we recover a more biblical vision of worship that encompasses not just our own story but also the Grand Story of Jesus and his followers in every time and place. This does not mean losing our distinctiveness or severing our historical roots; it simply means building on our unique strengths and learning from each other how to invite people into a more complete, and therefore more transforming, encounter with God. When we make the effort to transcend these divisions and worship God emotionally, volitionally, intellectually, and physically, we begin to taste the life-changing power of Experiential Worship.

THE STORY OF WORSHIP

Authentic worship is nothing less than a personal encounter with the living God. God comes to us and we respond; the mysterious and transforming intersection is what we call "worship." This intersection can happen anyplace and anytime we are loving God and seeking him: on a mountaintop, in the car, even in the shower. True worship is not limited to an event or a place but becomes more and more a lifestyle in which everything we do is an expression of our love for Jesus. As Louie Giglio, founder of the Passion worship festivals, writes, "Worshiping God is what we do as we respond to His mercy in our 'walking around life.' It's not the words I sing, but me I bring; I am the offering laid at Your feet, my steps the melody oh so sweet, all of me in praise of Thee."[1]

Furthermore, something unique and powerful can happen when we gather as a community to seek an encounter with God *together*. Jesus promised his special presence when we gather in his name (see Matthew 18:20). Although there is much more that comprises a life of following Jesus, this weekly gathering for worship is the cornerstone of the Christian community and the special calling of those who lead that community. To lead corporate worship is to show others the way to this divine intersection by both our role in the worship gathering and by our own example of worship.

As we lead others into these divine encounters, God is always the focus. What freedom it is to discover that worship is not about *us*! As a popular worship song says, "It's all about *you*, Jesus." However, biblical worship is bidirectional: God comes to us, and we respond by giving ourselves to God. That means that while God is the focus of worship, our own experience *does* matter because that is what empowers our response.

The experience of the worshiper is of particular concern to those of us who plan and lead worship gatherings. We have been entrusted with the responsibility of facilitating encounters in which God can transform us from self-centered consumers into true God-centered worshipers. Experiential Worship leaders do not propagate a self-absorbed church culture in which worship is centered on our own felt needs but instead facilitate experiences that move people to focus their worship on God alone. As people encounter God more fully, they will be empowered to give themselves more freely to God, offering their worship to him with heart, soul, mind, and strength.

OWNING UP TO OUR PRESENT STORY

Biblical worship is a life-changing encounter with God himself, moving us to give all that we are back to our Creator. However, we realize that these kinds of encounters are best-case scenarios and do not reflect the effect of typical worship services today. Even if we do occasionally witness key turning points taking place during our gatherings, far too rarely do we see in the lives of those who worship regularly the incremental changes that constitute an ongoing process of spiritual transformation.

In the majority of our churches, life-changing experiences, even incremental ones, are more the exception than the rule. If we are honest, we will admit that our services can easily slip into meaningless rote, driven more by habit than spiritual passion, and that many people attend every week and leave unchanged.

This worship impotence is not due to lack of effort. Most of us put tremendous energy into planning and leading meaningful worship experiences. Many are willing to make sacrifices and endure criticism in order to create an environment in which people can worship God and be touched by his Spirit. But for all our effort, the lack of actual changed lives can be a crushing disappointment to those who give so much.

The way out of this predicament is to rediscover the wide range of historical worship traditions and learn how to connect them to our emerging culture. We are in the midst of nothing less than an epochal transition, a tectonic social shift, a cultural revolution that is birthing a world we call "postmodern" because we can only describe what it is not. Like fish unaware of the sea they swim in, we have often planned and led worship without recognizing the impact of our changing cultural environment. But now the currents have shifted. No longer is the water flowing in the direction of the traditions we inherited. If we do not learn to navigate these new waters differently, we will be swept away by this relentless tide of cultural change.

The rediscovery of Experiential Worship is not just an optional diversion for those attracted to innovation and experimentation. It is a necessity for every ministry that seeks to live and share the good news of Jesus Christ in this emerging new world. The time has come to transcend the contemporary worship trends of the late twentieth century and go beyond the calls for "multisensory" or "postmodern" worship in the early part of the twenty-first. We need worship that is thoroughly biblical, post-contemporary, pre-traditional—worship that leads us into a more complete encounter with God.

How can we help our members consistently experience God more fully so that incremental transformation becomes the rule rather than the exception? How can we plan and lead worship gatherings that invite people to move beyond ritual and habit to giving themselves more completely to God? As we learn to create gatherings that encompass the full range of biblical worship and human experience, we will see lives profoundly changed through more complete encounters with God.

JESUS' STORY FOR WORSHIP

When we read biblical accounts of people worshiping God, we find them engaged on all four levels of human experience. Everyone who encounters God in the Bible walks away profoundly changed. Imagine what it would be like to worship like that! What if you worshiped God in a way that involved you physically, engaged you intellectually, moved you emotionally, and empowered you volitionally? It would be a more holistic, biblical kind of worship—the kind that God can use to continually change your life.

Once when Jesus was asked to name the greatest commandment, he gave a simple but profound answer that forms the basis for this kind of worship: "You shall love the Lord your God with all your heart, and with all your soul, and with all your mind, and with all your strength" (Mark 12:30). Worship based on Jesus' greatest commandment recaptures a biblical paradigm that brings the disparate stories of Christian faith together into one powerful dynamic and transforms the lives of those who experience it. This more biblical, more complete, more life-changing approach is what I call "Experiential Worship." Let's go sit at the feet of Jesus and discover what he has to teach us about this kind of worship.

Part One

THE GREATEST COMMANDMENT: EXPERIENTIAL WORSHIP IS NOT OPTIONAL!

Our message of the gospel came to you not in word only, but also in power and in the Holy Spirit and with full conviction.

1 THESSALONIANS 1:5

Chapter 1

WHY IS WORSHIP SO IMPORTANT?

LOVING GOD

Twenty years ago, I woke up in a hospital bed, trying to figure out why I was there. My face was covered with cuts, my hands were swollen, and my leg was encased in massive bandages. Gradually, as the fog cleared, I came to understand that I had miraculously survived a head-on collision with a semi at sixty miles an hour. Lying there, pondering the fact that logically I should be dead, questions of purpose and meaning took on a new relevance for me: *Why am I here? What is my purpose? When all is said and done, what will really matter in my life?* It's easy to go through life unconcerned about such issues when you assume things will go on as they are forever. But when naive assumptions shatter on the rocks of reality, every human being begins to search for deeper meaning.

It is no surprise that Rick Warren's book *The Purpose-Driven Life* was an instant best seller, because he directly addresses these questions. Who among us has not found himself asking these questions at different times in his life? And who among us has not marveled at the spiritual power and simple beauty of Jesus' answer: the Great Commandments? To love God with all we are and love our neighbor as ourselves (see Mark 12:28-34)—Jesus captures everything that matters in life with a phrase so simple a child can remember it.

Yet hearing and marveling are not enough. What does it really mean to love God? It is easier to imagine how to apply the second commandment because our "neighbor" is a tangible reality that we can see, touch, and love in concrete actions. But what about God? How do you love the invisible, ineffable, almighty Creator of the universe? At least the disciples had the historical Jesus—the fishermen could leave their nets to follow him (see Mark 1:18), Mary could wipe his feet with her hair (see John 12:3), and Peter could cut off the ear of a slave in Christ's defense (see John 18:10). But how are we to love the God we cannot touch or see? Jesus said that loving "one of the least of these" was a way of loving him (see Matthew 25:40), but that brings us back to the second commandment again.

Loving God with all of our heart, soul, mind, and strength can be expressed in anything we do that serves Jesus Christ and the kingdom of God. This encompasses all of our lives, from the simple and ordinary to the extravagant and sublime. Hopefully, we are all learning indirect ways of loving God by the way we live our lives every day. However, there is a way that we can express our love to God directly and specifically: worship. The beauty and wonder of worship is that it is the only thing we can give to God that he does not already have. Worship is the one thing we do exclusively to express our love to God.

People use the term *worship* to mean many things, including singing, programs, strategies, liturgies, and musical styles. However, true worship in the spirit of Jesus' Great Commandment is something much deeper and more profound. God comes to us through his Word in the power of the Spirit and offers us—among other things—love, truth, conviction, grace, forgiveness, comfort, exhortation, and guidance. When we see God for who he is and experience all that he offers, we respond in humility, gratitude, and faith with such acts as confession, repentance, commitment, adoration, thanksgiving, intercession, and celebration. Worship leader and songwriter Matt Redman describes worship as "revelation and response."[1] Notice that worship does not begin with us but finds its source in divine initiative: God reveals himself to us, and we respond to God. The intersection of these two dynamics is true worship, a transforming encounter in which God loves us and we love God with heart, soul, mind, and strength.

A BI-DIRECTIONAL ENCOUNTER WITH GOD

This kind of biblical worship moves us far beyond the singing we do on Sunday morning into a holistic encounter with God that engages all aspects of human experience. Thus, we begin to see that real worship—loving God—encompasses everything that happens in our weekly gatherings and overflows into everything we do the other six days of the week as well.

Some will object to the whole premise of Experiential Worship, pointing out that biblical worship calls us to focus our attention on *giving to* God rather than *getting from* God. Rick Warren writes, "The most common mistake Christians make in worship today is seeking an experience rather than seeking God."[2] Warren is right to point out that the attention of the true worshiper is always focused on God, not on self. However, to stop there is to offer only a partial understanding of worship. While genuine worship is always seeking to give to God, paradoxically we are also recipients of all that God is when we genuinely offer ourselves to him. This is what it means to say that worship is a bidirectional encounter with God.

Worship planners and leaders are responsible for facilitating experiences of God while directing people to focus on the God they are experiencing. Worship innovator Sally Morgenthaler captures this balance when she writes, "As a young worship leader, I focused on creating worship experiences, on making sure people felt they'd met God before they left. As a worship planner, I still ask the question *How are people going to encounter God in this time of worship?* But increasingly, I'm focusing on the God of our experience, not the experience itself."[3] The more we help people experience God in authentic ways, the more they will be empowered to respond by worshiping him with heart, soul, mind, and strength.

OUR DESIGN AND DESTINY

It is no coincidence that Jesus, when asked about the most important commandment, pointed us to loving God, because from the very beginning, the Bible tells us this is why we were created. The opening chapters of Genesis show us that Adam and Eve knew perfect joy in the Garden of Eden because they loved God with all their heart, soul, mind, and strength. But when God's sorrowful call "Where are you?" first echoed through the garden, we lost that intimate connection with our Creator and still struggle to recover the complete worship that was the very substance of paradise.

Just as the opening chapters of the Bible help us regain a vision for our original design, so the closing chapters give us a glimpse into our ultimate destiny in Christ. In the Revelation to John, we get a peek into the very throne room of God, where we find the four creatures, the twenty-four elders, and myriad angels all continually worshiping God as they sing, "To the one seated on the throne and to the Lamb be blessing and honor and glory and might forever and ever!" (Revelation 5:13). In the midst of all our speculation about the mysteries of heaven, there is one thing that is crystal clear: God has shown us our destiny in his eternal kingdom, and we discover it is glorious, extended worship!

THE PRIORITY OF WORSHIP

What is most important in your life? Priorities matter in a temporal existence because we only have a certain amount of time. Our priorities end up determining what we make time for and what we don't. I sometimes find myself frustrated at the end of a day because I realize I didn't make time for the things that mattered most. Unfortunately, there's no rewind button or "undo" command on the pull-down menus of our lives.

We were made to worship. No wonder the authors of the Westminster Confession wrote, "Man's chief and highest end is to glorify God, and fully to enjoy him forever."[4] When we love God with all of our heart, soul, mind, and strength, we are the closest we will ever be in this world to life in God's eternal kingdom.

This is why there is nothing that has a bigger impact on the people of your congregation than what happens in your weekly worship gatherings. Of course, Christian community and discipleship encompass much more than corporate worship, such as spiritual disciplines, small-group fellowship, ministry teams, missional service, and relational evangelism. However, it is encountering God together in worship that will shape and define the rest of those expressions of the body of Christ more than any other experience will.

Like the easily distracted Martha, we are being called to rediscover "the better part" that we have sometimes forgotten, to spend more time with Mary sitting at the feet of Jesus (see Luke 10:38-42). If worship is what we were created for, the most explicit expression of our love for God, and the most important aspect of our ministry, it becomes clear that authentically biblical worship will always invite people to encounter God and respond, as Jesus said, with all of their heart, soul, mind, and strength.

Chapter 2

WORSHIP AND IDENTITY

A LOOK IN THE MIRROR

In the movie *Hook*, Robin Williams portrays a grown-up Peter Pan returning to Neverland on a quest to rediscover his true identity. I love the scene in which the overgrown Pan is being examined by the Lost Boys. One of the youngest grabs ahold of Pan's fleshy face and stretches the skin until finally, with the joy of recognition, he exclaims, "Oh, *there* you are, Peter!" We all need help to see who we really are.

We are complex people. Created in God's image, we contain within us unimaginable potential for good. Yet broken by sin, we display a frightening and persistent propensity toward "the dark side." Anthropology is the study of human complexity. All religions offer their own kind of anthropology in an attempt to explain who we are in relationship to God. In a sense, the entire Bible is a narrative anthropology: the story that defines God's people.

However, within the Bible we find various anthropologies, different ways of describing human beings. Both the Old and New Testaments refer to the human being as "soul and body" (Isaiah 10:18; Matthew 10:28) or as "heart and soul" (Deuteronomy 4:29; Acts 4:32). Paul likes to describe human existence as the struggle between flesh and Spirit (see Romans 8:12-13). Sometimes the Scriptures refer to people as mind and body (see Ecclesiastes 11:10); "heart and mind" (Psalm 64:6); mind and spirit (see 1 Corinthians 14:14-15); soul, spirit, and heart (see Hebrews 4:12); or "spirit and soul and body" (1 Thessalonians 5:23).

This variety of descriptions demonstrates that words are symbols, pointing us to deeper realities that do not always fit the limited categories of human language. There is no one "right" term or phrase that defines who we are as God's children. The variety of books written to explain what is meant by these various terms demonstrates the elasticity of such words and categories.[1] It is important for us to approach anthropological terms with flexibility, recognizing that we are not dealing with simple, reducible categories of human existence but with metaphors that help us understand part of the mystery of human identity, even if "in a mirror, dimly" (1 Corinthians 13:12).

JESUS' ANTHROPOLOGY OF WORSHIP

When Jesus answered the scribe's insightful question about the greatest commandment, he was quoting the famous "Shema" from Deuteronomy 6:4-5, which was a prominent part of the liturgy in the Jewish synagogue at the time of Jesus and remains so today. The connection of this verse to worship was obvious to Jesus' first audience. It wasn't the novelty of this passage that stood out to them; it was the unique way that Jesus used it to sum up the Law. Jesus' radical insight was that loving and worshiping God encompasses at least the vertical component of life as it is meant to be.

In the Hebrew text that we have received, Deuteronomy 6:5 includes only three words describing human beings, translated "heart," "soul," and "might." In the standard ancient Greek translation of the Hebrew Scriptures (the Septuagint) this passage includes four words: heart, soul, mind, and strength. All three versions of Jesus' Greatest Commandment in the Gospels include the words *heart, soul,* and *mind,* but only two of these include the word *strength* (see Matthew 22:37-39; Mark 12:30-31; Luke 10:27). Again we see the biblical writers' flexibility in using words that can point us only to complex mysteries that defy the strict categories of vocabulary. The point of each combination of words is the same: we are to love God with *all* that we are, every fiber of our beings. Although we cannot be sure what version of Deuteronomy 6:5 Jesus was actually quoting, when we put these various versions together, it seems clear that he was referring to four facets of human existence: heart, soul, mind, and strength.

HEART

My wife, Pam, and I spent nearly two years of our engagement on separate continents. Unable to afford phone calls, I did something profoundly out of character for me: I wrote her letters. We each put pen to paper almost every day, and now we have a large box filled with the documentation of our early, passionate love for each other. It is both wonderful and a little embarrassing to read those letters today. The letters as well as the envelopes are covered with every imaginable form of the symbol for the human heart. This was our attempt to give graphic expression to the indescribable emotions that were welling up inside.

In our culture, the heart is our primary symbol for strong, positive emotions. One glimpse at a Hallmark store in February is enough to prove this point. Not so in biblical times. In the Bible, the word *heart* primarily points to the human will—that amazing and terrifying power of choice with which God has designed us. We can see this in passages such as Psalm 119:2: "Happy are those who keep his decrees, who seek him with their whole heart." Paul demonstrates this understanding of the word when he admonishes Christian slaves to do "the will of God from the heart" (Ephesians 6:6). The biblical authors envision the heart primarily as the place where human intention resides.

Although we usually think of the heart in terms of our feelings, in present-day evangelistic settings, we often invite people to "accept Jesus with your heart." By this, we are describing not an emotion but a concrete response of the will. Sometimes in the Bible, the word *heart* is simply meant to point to the deepest part of human experience or consciousness. But especially when combined with words such as *soul* and *mind*, it is clear that Jesus used the word *heart* in this context to describe our ability to decide and choose.

SOUL

"Daddy, what happens to us when we die?" What a great opportunity for Christian parents to reinforce the message of the gospel with their children. Perhaps we would say something along the lines of, "Well, when you die, your body goes down into the ground and your soul goes up to heaven to be with God forever." If this is our answer, we are actually schooling our children more in the pagan beliefs of Greek mythology than in biblical salvation! A more biblical response would be to explain how Jesus' death and resurrection accomplishes the redemption of all that we are, heart, soul, mind, and body (see Romans 8:19-25; 1 Corinthians 15:42-57).

Most people in our society today, including many Christians, use the term *soul* to describe a nonmaterial reality that comprises the immortal identity of individuals and survives physical death. This is essentially a Greek anthropology and is found nowhere in the Bible. The biblical writers use the term *soul* in various ways but primarily to describe the emotional aspect of human nature. We can see this in passages such as Psalm 35:9, "Then my soul shall rejoice in the LORD, exulting in his deliverance," and in Psalm 42:11, "Why are you cast down, O my soul, and why are you disquieted within me?" We see this same idea reflected in our modern use of the term *psychological*, which is based on the Greek word for the soul, *psuche*.

Sometimes the word *soul* in the Bible points to the deeper aspects of human existence. Sometimes it is paired with *heart* in a parallel structure rather than in contrast. However, when Jesus used the term *soul* along with *mind*, *body*, and *heart*, he was pointing to the vast range of our emotional experiences.

MIND

"A mind is a terrible thing to waste." In an age of scientific and technological triumph, we have elevated the mind to near divine status. From childhood, many of us were told that our value and future are directly dependent on how we develop and use our minds. Our educational system is tailored to reward a certain kind of logical and linear thinking. Anyone who has completed a degree in higher education has been schooled to think of the mind as the most important aspect of who we are. As medical advances have enabled us to revive people previously considered dead, we have come to define life and death based on brain activity.

In modern culture, we tend to think of the mind as a computer—an organ that stores, processes, and retrieves information. However, the biblical writers use the term *mind* to describe not just our ability to process information but also a consciousness that enables us to derive meaning and wisdom from that information. This biblical view of the mind emphasizes "knowing," which is both fact-based and relational.

The naive modern assumption that brainpower could somehow solve the deepest problems of human existence has been brutally discredited by the atrocities of the past century. In the postmodern culture of the twenty-first century there is a tendency to see the mind as a network that connects and interprets the various aspects of human experience and leads us toward deeper meaning. This is very similar to the biblical writers' use of the term *mind*. When Solomon asks for wisdom, God responds, "I now do according to your word. Indeed I give you a wise and discerning mind; no one like you has been before you and no one like you shall arise after you" (1 Kings 3:12). Paul describes Christian unity as being "of one mind" (Philippians 2:2) and Christian maturity as gaining "the mind of Christ" (1 Corinthians 2:16). When Jesus calls us to love God with our "mind," he is talking about a cognitive function that leads us to spiritual meaning.

STRENGTH

"Those are strong words." "That's a strong cup of coffee." "She has unusual strength of character." We use the word *strength* to describe the same trait in many different contexts. In Scripture, sometimes *strength* refers to personal determination, other times to moral conviction, but it is often connected to the physical aspect of human existence. Proverbs 20:29 uses this word to describe the aging process of the body: "The glory of youths is their strength, but the beauty of the aged is their gray hair." Sometimes lack of physical strength is described: "My strength fails because of my misery, and my bones waste away (Psalm 31:10). Even when physical strength is used as a spiritual metaphor, physical images are used: "But those who wait for the LORD shall renew their strength, they shall mount up with wings like eagles, they shall run and not be weary, they shall walk and not faint" (Isaiah 40:31).

Early opponents of Christianity ridiculed the scandalous claim that God had become a physical person in Jesus Christ. A piece of second-century anti-Christian graffiti in Rome depicts a crucified donkey and mocks a certain believer with the inscription "Alexamenos is worshipping his God."[2]

The ancient heresy of Docetism was born in the refusal to believe Jesus could be fully human. The gnostics went so far as to claim that physical existence is intrinsically evil and the goal of spiritual life is to escape our corporal state. The incarnational aspect of Christian faith has always been folly and a scandal to our conventional wisdom. We see these same ideas in the popular assumption that "spirituality" is somehow the opposite of "physicality." This is a profoundly unbiblical view. From the first moment of Creation in Genesis to the final apocalyptic re-Creation in Revelation, the Bible offers an unwavering affirmation of the goodness of the physical order and its direct connection to spiritual realities. It follows that any truly biblical anthropology will take the same inclusive view of the human body.

When Jesus calls us to love God with all we are, he not only includes our will, our emotions, and our intellect, but he also puts all of these aspects of our humanity in the context of our physical bodies. To love God with all your strength means to allow your body to give expression to the thoughts, feelings, and decisions that reflect the response of the whole person to God.

JESUS' ANTHROPOLOGY FOR WORSHIP

BIBLICAL TERM	HUMAN TRAIT	RESPONSE IN WORSHIP
Heart	Volitional	What we choose
Soul	Emotional	What we feel
Mind	Intellectual	What we think
Strength	Physical	What we do

SCRAMBLED EGGS, NOT LEGOS!

In the powerful movie *Good Will Hunting*, Matt Damon plays Will, a character who demonstrates the kind of anthropology that lies behind Jesus' Great Commandment. Will is a physically strong young man who possesses a phenomenal intellect. However, due to his abusive past, he suffers from a profound emotional paralysis that prevents him from making the necessary choices that would lead him to a fulfilling and productive life. With the help of a therapist, he is able to find the emotional healing he needs to embrace his unusual intellect. This healing empowers him to make some critical decisions that lead him out of the circumstances that have kept him utilizing only a tiny fraction of his potential and into a life filled with untold possibilities.

This is exactly what Jesus wants to do for us by helping us embrace the full range of human experience in worship. Jesus' Greatest Commandment is an invitation to worship God with our wills, our emotions, our intellects, and our bodies—an experience encompassing all that it means to be a human being. Throughout the rest of this book, we will explore what that kind of worship looks like, its power to transform lives, and how we can make those kinds of experiences a reality for more people.

It would be very tempting at this point to think of these four aspects of human existence as neat compartments that can be clearly defined and functionally categorized—something like a stack of Lego building blocks, with each part snapping onto the next. However, this image owes more to Greek philosophy than to the Bible.

All biblical anthropologies envision the human being as an integrated whole, not a collection of separable compartments. It's kind of like scrambled eggs. They're comprised of identifiable parts: yolks, whites, water, salt, and pepper. Yet once whipped and cooked, these various elements are impossible to separate. You cannot unscramble eggs! As we explore what it means to worship God with all of our heart, soul, mind, and strength, we would be wise to remember that these words are symbols that point to different aspects of what it means to be human and that a unique combination of all four are integrated and inseparable within every person.

Chapter 3

WORSHIP AND PERSONAL TRANSFORMATION

A WHOLE-PERSON GOD-ENCOUNTER

The red granite cliffs rose all around him, and the desert heat beat down like a camel driver's whip. He was a simple man, a man with a past, to be sure, but content with his station in life. Shepherding flocks in the barren Sinai was no cakewalk, but he had resigned himself to it. He did his job, minded his own business, and expected others to do the same.

This day was like any other, but then something happened that changed everything. He couldn't remember if he smelled the fire or heard it crackle, but there was no doubt about what he saw: a bush engulfed in flames—but not burning up! And then, in the shadow of that great mountain, an angel appeared to him—or was it God himself? "Moses, Moses."

He answered, "Here I am." God said, "Remove the sandals from your feet, for the place on which you are standing is holy ground." Then, standing there with the hot sand burning his feet, Moses heard the words that would change his life forever: "I am the God of your father, the God of Abraham, the God of Isaac, and the God of Jacob." (adapted from Exodus 3)

Face-to-face with a burning bush. Standing barefoot on holy ground. This is the stuff of an encounter with God. Why did Moses make such an impact on history? Was it his early days in Pharaoh's court? Was it the terrible mistake he made in taking a man's life? Was it the years of solitude spent in the wilderness? Certainly, all of these experiences were woven into the fabric of the man, but there is no doubt that it was Moses' face-to-face meeting with God that changed him and sent him on a collision course with destiny.

God-encounters both big and small change us. Why was this event so profound for Moses? Let's take a closer look at the nature of the experience.

First of all, it was a *physical* experience. Moses saw the burning bush with his eyes. He took off his sandals and felt the ground with his bare feet. God gave him Mount Horeb as a physical landmark along his way and the promise of a new land, flowing with milk and honey. For reassurance, God gave him tangible signs: a staff that changed shape, a hand that was made leprous and then made clean, and water that turned to blood (see Exodus 4:3-9).

Second, it was an *intellectual* experience. God explained his purpose for the people of Israel and Moses' role in freeing them from bondage. Moses asked how he would establish the authority of his calling, and God gave his personal name to back him up. God gave Moses a strategy for confronting Pharaoh and instructions on how to lead the people out of Egypt.

Third, it was an *emotional* experience. Moses hid his face in fear. He doubted his ability to lead. Patiently and persistently, God coaxed him out of fear and doubt into hope with persuasive promises and an inspiring vision of his future.

Finally, it was a *volitional* experience. God called Moses to respond with specific choices and concrete actions: "Remove the sandals from your feet . . . say to the Israelites . . . go and assemble the elders of Israel . . . go to the King of Egypt and say to him . . . now go . . ." (Exodus 3:5,14,16,18).

The miracle of the story is that he *did* go. This runaway murderer, who answered God with nothing but denials and excuses, did exactly what God called him to do: he led God's people out of bondage. How? By the power of an encounter with God that empowered him to respond with his heart, soul, mind, and body.

Later, at this same mountain, Moses again came face-to-face with his Lord, but this time the impact of the experience was visible. Exodus 34:29-35 tells us that when he came down from the mountain after receiving the tablets of the Law from God, Moses' face was shining with reflected glory. Moses would put a veil over his face when he was with the people and then remove it when he was in the presence of God.

Different interpretations of the veil have been given, but Paul explains that Moses was hiding the fact that the glory of this dramatic encounter was fading from his face (see 2 Corinthians 3:13). By contrast, Paul describes the ongoing process of change that takes place as we encounter God regularly in Christ: "All of us, with unveiled faces, seeing the glory of the Lord as though reflected in a mirror, are being transformed into the same image from one degree of glory to another; for this comes from the Lord, the Spirit" (2 Corinthians 3:18).

This is an important reminder to us that transformation is a process. Too often, we put all our emphasis on a dramatic and sensational encounter with God, forgetting that lasting life-change comes in an ongoing, step-by-step process. For this reason, Experiential Worship is not so much about providing once-in-a-lifetime experiences for people as it is about providing regular opportunities for authentic encounters with God.

FROM ENCOUNTER TO TRANSFORMATION

We all encounter God every day, whether we realize it or not: the sun pouring through the window as we wake up, the food that nourishes us for the activities of our day, the love of family and friends with whom we share our lives, the joy of productive labor in God's kingdom, and the comfort of sleep as we are restored for a new day. God is there, available to us, inviting us to encounter him in the ordinary things of our everyday lives.

The same is true of our worship gatherings. Every time we come together for Christian worship, God is present. Yet we know that often worship services produce little or no perceptible life-change in the people who attend. What is it that makes an encounter with God life-changing? The question is not whether *God* is present to *us*; the question is how present *we* are to God. In his famous prayer "Late Have I Loved You," St. Augustine admits, "All the time you were with me, but I was not with you."[1] This raises the question "Does the particular form of our worship really help people to be present to God in a transforming way?"

During my academic training, I had the opportunity to live and study in Jerusalem for an entire school year. It was an amazing experience for numerous reasons, one of which was the exposure to so many different forms of worship. I have always been fascinated by the varied ways that people worship God, and over the years I have made it a goal to experience as many different types of worship as possible.

That year, during the Week of Prayer for Christian Unity, the various churches of Jerusalem organized a series of ecumenical services. Each service was to be held in a different kind of church each evening from a Sunday to a Sunday. I made it a point to attend, and my eyes were opened to the incredible diversity of worship forms that comprise our faith. Some services were more formal and helped me to experience the mysterious transcendence of God. Others were more personal and drew me into the intimate immanence of God. Some were visual in nature, the worship space covered in vivid icons. Others were very musical, inviting the people to sing and express their love for God outwardly.

I was amazed most by the Ethiopian Orthodox service. The intricately decorated sanctuary was a round domed building with a small house-shaped structure standing at the very center, enclosing the altar. This smaller structure had open windows and doorways on all four sides. The congregation stood all the way around the perimeter of the worship space as the priests went in and out of all four doorways accessing the altar, swinging incense holders, and singing the liturgy. Most amazing to me was that they sang not only the entire liturgy but the Scripture readings and the sermon as well! As bizarre as this might seem to American Protestant Christians, this is the form of worship that is familiar to Ethiopian Orthodox Christians. I'm positive that worship services with electric guitars, video projectors, or children's sermons would seem even more bizarre to them!

That week of diverse worship gatherings opened my eyes to see that for all the varied forms of Christian worship, there is one common goal they share: to help people give themselves to God in such a way that God is glorified and they are changed. But it also opened my eyes to see that the main reason people are not being transformed in many of our worship services is because we are each offering our own derivative portion of worship rather than a full range of experiences as envisioned in Jesus' Great Commandment.

This does not mean that we all have to learn Ethiopian or start singing the Scriptures, but imagine what could happen if we began to open our eyes to the broader range of approaches to worship and the experiences they elicit! Sadly, worship in Spirit and truth, that mighty river of Living Water that Jesus promised the Samaritan woman at the well (see John 4:1-26), has been siphoned off into so many tributaries that they have become tiny rivulets, unable to move the heart and touch the soul.

Richard Foster offers us a different vision in his prophetic book *Streams of Living Water*:

> Today a mighty river of the Spirit is bursting forth from the hearts of women and men, boys and girls. It is a deep river of divine intimacy, a powerful river of holy living, a dancing river of jubilation in the Spirit, and a broad river of unconditional love for all peoples. . . . The astonishing new reality in this mighty flow of the Spirit is how sovereignly God is bringing together streams of life that have been isolated from one another for a very long time.[2]

Foster's vision is a call to learn from each other and regain the full historical content of our biblical faith so that the Spirit might move dynamically through the various expressions of Christianity once again.

STREAMS OF WORSHIP TRADITION

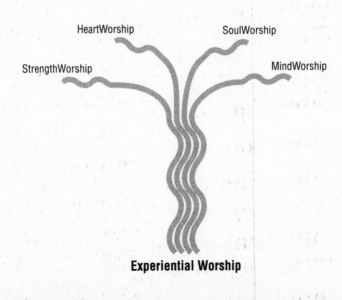

HeartWorship   SoulWorship

StrengthWorship   MindWorship

Experiential Worship

This does not mean that we lose the distinctiveness of our varied traditions. To lose that would be to amputate essential limbs from the wider body of Christ. We need a broad variety of churches and various kinds of worship experiences in order to reach the great diversity of people and cultures that make up the emerging world that is becoming our reality. The key is that each community of faith utilizes its unique combination of resources, context, and history to invite people into a more complete experience of God that is empowered by the various streams of Christian tradition.

EMERGING CONVERGENCE

We can see that Foster's dream is beginning to come true in the emerging worship movement today. Out of a combination of Spirit-led innovation and missional desperation, we see varied traditions learning from each other and offering a more complete biblical worship experience. Evangelical churches are rediscovering the sacraments and inviting people into the mystery of God through the creative use of ancient liturgical practices. Liturgical churches are learning to embrace culturally relevant music, cutting-edge technology, and more effective modes of communication to reach new generations. Bible-teaching churches are making more room for the power and work of the Holy Spirit. Charismatic churches are discovering the strength of a doctrinal foundation. Grace-based churches are beginning to teach intentional discipleship. Discipling churches are discovering grace as the basis of true obedience.

The growing number of books being published and conferences being held around the world on "The Emerging Church" are testimony to this exciting and experimental quest to reimagine the church for a postmodern world. Dan Kimball's Vintage Faith Church is a perfect example of this kind of church. Coming from a conservative Bible-church background, this innovative community is bringing together elements from its strong evangelical heritage with ancient traditions familiar in more liturgical churches and current trends from the emerging culture.[3] Developing Experiential Worship in my own mainline liturgical context, I find myself arriving at almost the exact same place Dan Kimball does but coming from the completely opposite end of the historical spectrum.

This confluence of traditions is producing not congregational clones but unique communities through which the Spirit is flowing with greater power. In his well-researched study *The Younger Evangelicals*, Robert Webber compellingly describes this promising phenomenon prevalent among the emerging generation of leaders and an approach to worship he calls "convergence."[4] As the streams of various traditions come together to create more complete worship experiences, we will see lives changed like never before.

BEYOND PHOTO ALBUMS

When I was sixteen years old, my sister and I went on the adventure of our young lives: a month-long car trip through Germany, Italy, Austria, and Switzerland. We had wonderful experiences together, saw some of the most significant monuments of European history, and explored beautiful vistas from the Italian Riviera to the Swiss Alps. I took picture after picture of grand castles and ancient churches, sunlit beaches and snowcapped peaks. When we got home, I could hardly wait to open the newly developed prints and share my experiences with family and friends.

However, my excitement quickly turned to disappointment as I looked through the photos. It wasn't that they didn't turn out—they were fine. But as I looked through the pictures, I realized that photographs could not convey the experience. Sure, they captured the shapes and the colors we had seen. But they were only two-dimensional miniatures, while the actual experience had been profoundly three-dimensional on a grand scale.

Furthermore, the photos could not convey the sounds, smells, and senses that went with the images: the ringing of the bells at St. Mark's in Venice, the heat of the stones in the Colosseum, or the queasiness of a Swiss mountain road. But even if I could have shown my friends and family a holographic video with simulated environmental stimuli, nothing could convey the emotions, thoughts, and decisions that the actual experience evoked; you just had to be there. The only one who really understood the pictures was my sister because she had been there with me.

Too often our worship services are like showing photos to people who have never been there. At first they seem to enjoy what we show them (though they quickly get bored), but they are missing out on the realities to which the symbols point. As our culture is changing, people are less and less tolerant of our photo itineraries. There are too many other opportunities for them to experience something real. If we would stop boring people with two-dimensional photo albums and learn to take them with us on the actual adventure of authentic encounters with God, we would rediscover the joy and power of truly biblical worship.

The film *Memento* tells the story of a man who is trying to investigate his wife's murder. The only problem is that since the incident, he has lost his ability to retain any memories. Rather than try to describe this dilemma to us, the filmmaker has constructed the story with a series of scenes put together in reverse order; it begins at the end and finishes with the beginning. The result is that the viewer is thrown into the same dilemma as the main character: trying to piece together the mystery while constantly not knowing who people are and why things are happening.

The power of *Memento* is that it doesn't just *tell* us a story; it invites us to actually *experience* the story. Likewise, the power of Experiential Worship is that it doesn't just *tell* us about God; it invites us to actually *experience* God. Richard Foster begins his chapter on the spiritual discipline of worship by stating, "To worship is to experience Reality, to touch Life. It is to know, to feel, to experience the resurrected Christ in the midst of the gathered community."[5] This is what Paul described when he recalled the life-changing experience of worship he shared with the Thessalonian Christians: "Our message of the gospel came to you not in word only, but also in power and in the Holy Spirit and with full conviction" (1 Thessalonians 1:5).

THE CULTURAL MANDATE

If we are committed to helping people experience God today, we will go far beyond the latest techniques to the core of what worship is really about. We will learn whole new languages. Like those brave cross-cultural missionaries who have gone before us, we will become ongoing students of emerging cultures, continually interpreting and explaining the context of our particular ministries. We will rediscover the arts as a means of conveying the infinite to the finite and unleash artists to share their gifts with the community. We will seek to understand personality types and learning styles and the impact of different modes of communication. We will utilize the latest technology as the vernacular of our time. We will learn from the whole spectrum of Christian tradition in order to renew and invigorate our own stream of the faith. We will break out of our comfort zones and explore all God has for us on what Brian McLaren calls "the other side" of this postmodern cultural revolution.[6]

Radically changing our approach to planning and leading worship is not an option in this time of radical change; it is a matter of life and death. According to George Barna, "Among adults who regularly attend church services, one half admit that they haven't experienced God's presence in the past year."[7] And this in the midst of an emerging culture for which experience is everything! Leonard Sweet, expert on emerging culture and faith, lists "experiential" as the first of four keys to ministry in this new world. He writes, "Moderns want to figure out what life's about. Postmoderns want to experience what life is, especially experience life for themselves. Postmoderns are not willing to live at even an arm's-length distance from experience. They want life to explode all around them."[8]

Experiential Worship is not just another ministry fad, not just another clever technique; it is nothing less than the rediscovery of biblical worship, worship according to the Greatest Commandment of Jesus. It is the kind of worship that fueled the passions of the apostolic church, and it is the kind of worship people are crying out for in our time. The rest of this book offers ideas and suggestions, lessons learned from my own mistakes, and wisdom gained from the insights of others. My goal and passion in writing this is that we might help each other find our way through this bewildering and constantly changing landscape to a place where we no longer *tell* people about God but rather invite them to *experience* God for themselves.

During a particularly challenging and exhilarating climb to Angel's Landing in Zion National Park, I was overwhelmed by the beauty and wonder of a place that cannot be described but must be experienced. As we were leaving the park, I noticed a promotional slogan on one of the signs: "Experience Your National Parks."

That's it. No more photo albums; no more secondhand trip itineraries. The trail is steep and treacherous, not for the faint of heart, but it leads to a view that words can't describe—a place where lives are being changed from one degree of glory to another. Jesus invites us to follow him on this narrow road that leads to life!

Part Two

STRENGTH WORSHIP:
ENGAGING AND TRANSFORMING THE BODY

---

*Present your bodies as a living sacrifice, holy and acceptable to God,
which is your spiritual worship.*

ROMANS 12:1

Chapter 4

PHYSICAL MATTERS!

A STORY OF PLACE

After twenty-two hours of driving, getting out of the driver's seat felt like a luxury. Stretching and groaning, I began to walk down the path toward the lake. As I took in a deep breath, I felt a lifetime of memories flooding over me: the smell of ponderosa pines, the feel of summer heat, the sound of rocks crunching underfoot, the sight of endless blue shimmering through the trees. Like a time machine, those sensations sent my mind reeling through the years to countless days I had spent in that most special of places.

My grandfather bought the property sight unseen in 1946 while he was far from home, completing his service to our country. He didn't need to see it to know that waterfront property on glacier-cut Flathead Lake was an investment in a legacy. There he built a small cabin, where my father spent his boyhood summers playing on the rock beach that had been shaped and smoothed by eons of endless waves. I was born a stone's throw from this place, so I experienced its wordless beauty long before conscious memory began. Every summer of my boyhood was spent on that same beach, swimming in those same waves. To this day, our annual summer vacation in Montana is the highlight of every year.

As I stepped onto the beach, I could hear my two boys coming down the path behind me like a freight train running wild. They too have spent every summer vacation of their lives playing on that same beach, swimming in these same waves. I dived into the crystal-clear water, and felt my body enveloped in a perfect slipcover of cool refreshment. Gliding to the surface, sputtering for air, I could hear the shouting and laughter of two boys in paradise. Sounds of my sister's giggle came to me, floating across the water and through the years—an echo of our childhood games played in those pristine waters.

My words cannot express the beauty and wonder of that place. You would have to be there to understand. Words cannot convey to you the real significance of that spot, because it is comprised of a lifetime—no, generations—of experiences residing not so much in my mind but in the very fiber of my being. It is the smells, sights, and sounds of that place—the experience of physically being there—that triggers these memories and reminds me of who I am, where I have come from. For me, it has become a sacred place.

SACRED PLACES

We have lost our sense of sacred place. Ever since the temple curtain was torn in two, we have celebrated that God is not confined to a house made with human hands. Ever since the Day of Pentecost, we have known that wherever we are, whatever we are doing, God is present to us, ready to meet us and commune with us. On the other hand, we sometimes forget that our biblical faith is rooted in specific places: Adam and Eve were created in the Garden of Eden, Noah's ark came to rest on Mount Ararat, Abraham and Sarah were called from Ur of the Chaldees to the land of Canaan. Our Christian faith is centered on a historical event that happened in a particular place: the death of Jesus on a rock called Golgotha and his resurrection from a nearby tomb.

Traveling to the Holy Land is a reminder that God comes to us through the physical realities he created. Of course, God is no more present in Jerusalem than he is to you right now. However, there is something powerful about physically being in the actual places where sacred things transpired. When Pam and I lived in Jerusalem, our apartment was in the heart of the walled Old City, directly across from the ancient church that is built over the rock of Golgotha and the empty tomb of Joseph of Arimathea. Early each morning, before going off to my studies, I would stop in the small chapel at Golgotha for my quiet time. Kneeling there on stones worn smooth by centuries of knees, smelling the incense, seeing the candlelit icons, touching the actual rock where Jesus died, I would experience God's presence in a unique and wonderful way. The reality of Jesus' suffering, the precious gift of atonement, and the power of his resurrection all became real to me in a way that reading about it could not convey.

I am not suggesting you need to go to the Holy Land to encounter God, but I am saying that when we are engaged on a physical level, we experience God more completely. I am beginning with the physical dimension of Experiential Worship because I believe it is the aspect Protestants and Evangelicals have forgotten most. While the Reformers were right to condemn the superstition and idolatry that can become connected to physical expressions of worship, I believe we've thrown the baby out with the bathwater. As we regain a biblical understanding of sacred space and the spirituality of physicality, we will learn to create worship gatherings where people can experience God with their bodies as well as their hearts, souls, and minds.

A SACRED CREATION

From the beginning, God expressed himself through physical reality, and his Word did not just remain an idea but actually became what it described. God created our physical world and he specifically told us its value: "it was very good" (Genesis 1:31). After sin marred that goodness, God did not give up on the world he created but began working to redeem it. God made covenants with his people and used physical elements as signs of those renewed relationships: the rainbow with Noah, circumcision with Abraham, tablets of stone with Moses, animal sacrifices with Aaron. But somehow these signs were not enough. No matter how much patience God showed, we were not able to live in these covenants, even with their physical signs, so God went one step further.

I wonder if Mary comprehended the words of the angel with her mind before she felt the baby inside of her. How could she comprehend it? It was physically impossible; she had never been with a man, yet her body began to tell her differently. Maybe the first sign of her pregnancy was nausea or fatigue or a growing waistline, but steadily it became impossible to deny.

"And now, you will conceive in your womb and bear a son" (Luke 1:31). Mary was coming to know the truth with her body: the Creator of the universe was entering into creation.

Did the shepherds comprehend the words of the angel with their minds before they saw the child? It would have been easy for them to deny what they had heard and seen in the sky that night. After all, it could have been just a dream or maybe a falling star. But it was impossible to explain away once they found what the angel had told them they'd find, "a child wrapped in bands of cloth and lying in a manger" (Luke 2:12). He was right there physically before their very eyes: a little child they could touch with their hands, hear with their ears, and see with their eyes. It was an experience that moved them so deeply that they "returned, glorifying and praising God for all they had heard and seen, as it had been told them" (Luke 2:20). God was making himself known through the very things he had created.

God didn't just *tell* us about himself; he *showed* himself to us. God entered into creation itself and became atoms and molecules, a tiny baby, a full-grown man. The incarnation is God's definitive statement on the sacred character of redeemed creation. Jesus is the ultimate affirmation of our physical reality because in him, God became physical to redeem us, hearts, souls, minds, and bodies. It is not only Jesus' physical existence but also the very nature of his ministry that points to the value of our bodies. Jesus did not sit in some ivory tower, proclaiming words of wisdom for all to hear. No, he spent his time rubbing shoulders with so-called sinners, giving fishermen unorthodox advice, and improving the wine list at wedding parties. His ministry largely consisted of touching the hurting and healing the sick. He demonstrated his deep concern for people's bodily well-being by his actions and explained that such physical transformation is a sign of God's coming kingdom (see Luke 4:16-18).

Above all, we see the sacred character of the physical in the fact that Jesus' own body became the means of our redemption. John the Baptist rightly identified Jesus early in his ministry as the sacrificial "Lamb of God" (John 1:29). It was Jesus' body hanging on a cross that achieved atonement for all of humanity. It was the reality of his resurrected body that vanquished the power of death itself. Paul makes it clear that Jesus' death and resurrection not only opened the way for our salvation but also for the redemption of the entire physical order: "The creation itself will be set free from its bondage to decay and will obtain the freedom of the glory of the children of God" (Romans 8:21).

Even the Resurrection underscores the enduring importance of the physical. The risen Christ was not some kind of nonmaterial "ghost" but a gloriously transformed physical being: Matthew told us that the women took hold of Jesus' feet when they saw him; Luke told us that Jesus broke bread with the disciples in Emmaus; John described the breakfast Jesus shared with them on the beach. Many have falsely assumed Jesus' mysterious appearances and disappearances in the resurrection accounts imply a nonmaterial being. C. S. Lewis points out that a body would pass through apparently "solid" materials if it were *more* substantive rather than *less*.[1] When you drop a pebble in a glass of water, it sinks to the bottom because rock is more solid than water. Therefore, the fact that the resurrected Christ could pass through doors and walls implies that he was *more* physical, not *less*.

Lewis vividly illustrates this biblical teaching in his allegory *The Great Divorce*, which depicts a bus tour from hell to the outskirts of heaven. The inhabitants of hell are semitransparent, lacking substantive existence, while the inhabitants of heaven are described as "solid spirits." One of the travelers from hell describes his first impression of heaven's outskirts:

> It was the light, the grass, the trees that were different; made of some different substance, so much solider than things in our country that men were ghosts by comparison. Moved by a sudden thought, I bent down and tried to pluck a daisy which was growing at my feet. The stalk wouldn't break. I tried to twist it, but it wouldn't twist. I tugged till the sweat stood out on my forehead and I had lost most of the skin off my hands. The little flower was hard, not like wood or even like iron, but like diamond.[2]

The farther these "ghosts" venture into heaven, the more substantive and real everything becomes. If we base our images of God's eternal kingdom on the biblical accounts of Jesus' resurrection, we will imagine, as Lewis did, a reality where the physical and the spiritual are complete and completely integrated.

When the first-century Christians in Corinth were busy trying to separate their spirituality from their physicality, Paul had to remind them in the clearest possible terms that, like the risen Christ, we will be resurrected with renewed bodies (see 1 Corinthians 15). The early church recognized the importance of this point by including the phrase "I believe in the resurrection of the body" in the Apostles' Creed. But the spiritual value of the body is not only a future promise. Paul points out that the indwelling presence of the Holy Spirit establishes once and for all the sacred character of the redeemed human body here and now: "Or do you not know that your body is a temple of the Holy Spirit within you, which you have from God, and that you are not your own? For you were bought with a price; therefore glorify God in your body" (1 Corinthians 6:19-20). Truly biblical spirituality is never divorced from our physicality but always embraces the body as a sacred instrument of worship designed to glorify God. This is why Dallas Willard devotes an entire chapter of *Renovation of the Heart*, his landmark study of spiritual formation, to the topic of "transforming the body." He says, "For good or evil, the body lies right at the center of the spiritual life."[3]

THE BODY IN WORSHIP

Inviting people to worship God with their bodies is not a new idea. Throughout the Bible, worship is always described in physical terms. Biblical terminology itself reflects this; both the Hebrew and Greek words for *worship* literally mean "to fall down prostrate before someone." Many worship services today involve people's bodies from only the neck up, but biblical worship has always been a whole-body experience. Moses lay prostrate before God for forty days and nights (see Deuteronomy 9:9); Ezekiel threw himself on the ground while interceding for the people (see Ezekiel 11:13); Peter fell down before Jesus in recognition of his divinity (see Luke 5:8).

The Psalms, our biblical guidebook for worship, continually invites us into various physical expressions of worship: "*Clap* your hands, all you peoples; *shout* to God with loud songs of joy" (Psalm 47:1); "O come, let us worship and *bow down*, let us *kneel* before the LORD, our Maker!" (Psalm 95:6); "Come, bless the LORD, all you servants of the LORD, who *stand* by night in the house of the LORD! *Lift up your hands* to the holy place, and bless the LORD" (Psalm 134:1-2); and "Let them praise his name with *dancing*, making melody to him with tambourine and lyre" (Psalm 149:3).[4] Obviously, David and the other psalmists understood the body as an indispensable instrument of worship. If they were not afraid to call people to physical acts of worship, why are we?

One of the most vivid examples of using the whole body as an instrument of praise took place when David returned the sacred ark of the covenant to the Holy City: "David and all the house of Israel were dancing before the LORD with all their might, with songs and lyres and harps and tambourines and castanets and cymbals" (2 Samuel 6:5). How would we react if such overt, physical acts of worship suddenly broke out in our highly controlled services? I think many of us would have a response similar to that of David's wife Michal, who, when David danced before the Lord a few months later, "despised him in her heart" (2 Samuel 6:16).

Or maybe it is just those physical acts that are not familiar to us that would elicit judgment. Those who kneel in worship tend to look down on those who lift up their hands, and vice versa. I love David's reaction to Michal's disdain: he told her, "I will make myself yet more contemptible than this" (2 Samuel 6:22). Worship leader and songwriter Matt Redman invites us to respond with this same kind of holy boldness. In his insightful book *The Unquenchable Worshipper*, Redman encourages us to become "undignified worshipers" who are unashamed to give our whole selves, including our bodies, to God in worship, no matter what others might think.[5]

All of us have embraced the ears as receptors of God in worship. We listen to Scripture readings, sermons, prayers, and music. Most of us have embraced the vocal cords as a bodily instrument of worship. We sing praises to God, pray out loud, and respond vocally with creeds, declarations, tongues, or liturgies, depending on our tradition. Imagine how those who cannot hear or speak would experience your worship gathering. Would they have any opportunities to receive the message and respond?

There is so much more to the body than ears and vocal cords. It makes sense that we are rarely changed by encounters with God in our services—we are only engaging God with a small portion of our bodies.

How liberating it could be to return to a more biblical view of the human body and its role in worship. Imagine the freedom that would come if we learned to set aside our fears of what others might think, go outside our comfort zones, and develop worship experiences that invite people to glorify God with all of their physical strength.

PHYSICAL WORSHIP

I can vividly remember that period in life when my feet did not touch the floor as I sat in the pew at church. My legs dangled freely over the edge and swung back and forth almost effortlessly. No matter how many times my mom reminded me to stop, it was as if my legs had a mind of their own—I literally couldn't stop them from moving. Then my legs grew long enough so that, while they did not yet reach the floor, they did reach the back of the next pew. Now every time I swung my legs forward, they would just barely brush the hymn rack in front of me. *Swish, swish*—it made such a cool sound! My poor mother. How difficult it must have been to deal with a fidgety boy in a church culture where physical movement was frowned upon. There is a reason the Lutheran tradition I grew up in is sometimes referred to as the "frozen chosen"!

In that culture, worship is viewed primarily as a neck-up activity: we worship with our brains and our vocal chords. The rest of the body is expected to stay pretty much motionless. For a physically oriented person, that's like worshiping in a straitjacket! It was in youth group that I learned the whole body is an instrument of praise. There the culture was different. We were encouraged to move around while we worshiped, to use our hands to clap and do hand motions. Our youth director, Dave, liked to say, "If you're happy, why don't you let your face know?" That was a novel idea to many of us, but when we tried it, we liked it!

What you do with your body has a direct and immediate impact on your thoughts, emotions, and decisions. Wherever you are right now, put down this book, stand up, and stretch. Go ahead, do it. Done? Notice how you feel. Your mind is clearer; you feel better; you are ready to read more. Your body affects your heart, soul, and mind. When we kneel, fold our hands, and bow our heads, we tend to feel humbled, our thoughts turn inward, we find ourselves more able to submit to God. When we stand, look upward, and stretch our open palms to the sky, the movement tends to lift our emotions, focus our thoughts on God, and direct us toward thanks and praise.

There is a reason we usually teach children to close their eyes, fold their hands, and bow their heads when they pray. These are physical postures that help us focus all that we are on God. It doesn't mean this is the only posture for prayer. In fact, the typical posture for prayer in the time of the New Testament was to stand, lift up your hands, and look toward the sky. In her book on imaginative prayer, *God Encounter*, Lisa Tawn Bergren suggests, "If you're used to praying with head bowed, try laying prostrate on the floor. Bored with that? Try kneeling. I myself like to spread out on my back, with arms stretched wide, palms facing up . . . literally open and vulnerable beneath His gaze."[6] There is no one right posture for prayer or for worship. Each physical posture and motion affects us differently. When we learn to worship God physically, we discover that our bodies can help our hearts, souls, and minds to love God more completely.

When meeting with couples for premarital counseling, I always spend time going over the basic principles of active listening. I like to demonstrate the impact of body language on communication by turning my upper body away from the couple while they are talking and by looking out the window with my arms crossed and my fingers tapping restlessly. No matter how intently I might be listening to them, they feel ignored. The same is true about the way we use our bodies in worship: it will either help or hinder our experience of God. No matter what our tradition, if we help people learn to use their bodies as instruments of praise, we will lead them to a whole new depth of Experiential Worship.

LEARNING TO WORSHIP PHYSICALLY

Developing a broader repertoire of physical postures and movements in worship will help us encounter God more fully and keep us from falling into ruts and rote habits. Although I am not Pentecostal, I love to raise my hands while I sing to God. In fact, I have found a variety of hand movements helpful: when I am singing about my heart, I place my palms over my chest; when I am asking God for something, I hold out my cupped hands to receive; when I am confessing my sins in a song, I fold my hands and bow my head; when I am expressing God's glory and wonder, I lift both palms upward.

Likewise, I am not Roman Catholic or Orthodox, but I often use the ancient practice of crossing myself as a physical reminder of my baptism and God's presence with me. When I make the sign of the cross by touching a finger to my forehead, then my chest, then my left shoulder, then my right, I am physically reminded that I am God's child, saved by his grace, and that he has sealed me with the Holy Spirit forever. Other postures that help me include kneeling, or even bowing prostrate on the floor, as an expression of humility and repentance; and standing, moving back and forth, and looking upward toward the cross when singing songs of celebration.

By suggestion and example, we can help people discover and develop their own repertoire of physical worship. Gentle invitations and modeling during worship can help people try things they otherwise would never experience. In my church, we sometimes invite people to try a symbolic "prayer posture" as a physical act of worship. In gatherings focused on the power of God, we kneel with one hand outstretched to ask for God's strength. In gatherings focused on God's love, we stand with hands crossed over our hearts to express what words cannot. In gatherings focused on God's righteousness, we lift both hands above our heads, forming the shape of a chalice so that God might pour his goodness into us. Physical postures like these can constitute worship as significant as any song or prayer.

Learning to worship God with our bodies is a process. If we challenge ourselves as pastors and worship leaders to model this aspect of worship for our congregation, we can help them to grow in this area. Some of us will do this naturally; others will find it more difficult. There is no one right way to do it. Trying new things is never easy, but it is necessary if we want to deepen our experience of God. The more we get the focus off ourselves and onto God, the more we will be free to become "undignified worshipers" in the tradition of David.

If physical worship is new to your congregation, it will be especially important to be a careful student of your own church's culture and determine how to teach and lead your people into this biblical aspect of worship. Go slowly, communicate well, and allow people the freedom to participate at their chosen level. Don't pressure or intimidate people into certain physical expressions of worship. Always invite them to try it in their own way. Give them freedom and an example to follow. Additionally, always consider the newcomer. Paul instructs us to express our worship in a way that invites unbelievers into our midst so that they might experience God. Then, Paul says, "That person will bow down before God and worship him, declaring, 'God is really among you'" (1 Corinthians 14:25). As long as they are given the freedom to participate or not participate as they feel comfortable, newcomers will be drawn to worship God if they know we are genuinely glorifying God with our bodies.

THE BODY AS A SENSORY NETWORK

One of the reasons it is so critical that we engage people physically in worship is that the body is intricately interconnected with all the other aspects of who we are. Sometimes the Holy Spirit chooses to communicate directly with the soul, heart, or mind, but more often, God engages these aspects of human experience through the body. The complex interconnectedness of physical, psychological, and spiritual realities is well documented by scientific studies. You know from experience that if you are not feeling well physically, it affects your thinking, your feelings, and your decisions. Our body is the gateway to our hearts, minds, and souls.

All worship begins on the physical level. If people don't actually attend our worship gatherings, they cannot be changed through them. Like the old saying "Half of winning is just showing up," a person's physical presence is the starting point for any corporate worship experience. Once a person's body is present in our worship space, the rest of who they are is now available to experience God. This is where the senses come in.

When planning and leading worship, think of the physical senses as portals to human experience. How are people moved to tears? Maybe by watching a poignant drama (eyes). How do people come to understand a freeing truth about God? Maybe by listening to a well-written song that reinforces the sermon (ears). How do people begin to make different choices that honor God? Maybe by getting up out of their seats and carrying out symbolic acts during worship. Each of the physical senses provides a powerful connection to all of the other aspects of who we are.

You cannot lead people in worship without involving the senses at some level. Sitting motionless and listening to a sermon with your eyes closed requires at least the sense of hearing. However, the more senses we involve and the more significantly we engage those senses, the more compelling an experience we can facilitate. A worship gathering in which people not only are hearing potent truths but also seeing vivid images, feeling strong emotions, touching substantive realities, tasting nourishing flavors, and even smelling symbolic aromas has much greater potential for becoming a transforming encounter.

Chapter 5

Engaging the Senses in Worship

The Power of Sensory Experience

Waiting in line had turned anticipation to impatience, so when we were finally ushered in, I strapped myself into the seat with gusto. I found myself blinking in the sudden darkness as the lights went out and the music came on. There was an audible gasp as the seats lurched forward and up. The huge curved screen seemed twice as big once we were hanging in front of it like ripe fruit on a tree. Then, suddenly, we were flying! The ground dropped away and we barely cleared the tops of the trees. With wind in my face, I could smell the blossoms on the fruit trees and hear the river rushing below us. My stomach did a flip-flop as we banked left, then right, and dropped into a little canyon. The beauty of the scenery was awe-inspiring and the feeling of soaring freely over it was truly a thrill. When the seats dropped down and the lights came back on, it was hard to believe this had been only a ride at a theme park.

I love roller coasters and adventure rides, but "Soarin' Over California" is my favorite attraction at Disney's California Adventure theme park. Although you never leave the darkened building, all your physical senses tell you that you have just taken an amazing hang-glider flight over the most beautiful scenery and interesting attractions of California. You can see it, hear it, smell it, and feel it in your gut. It's amazing how your senses alone can evoke an intense experience. The more senses we engage and the more vividly we engage them, the more powerful the experience.

HEARING WORSHIP

One of Jesus' favorite sayings was "Let anyone with ears to hear listen!" (Mark 4:9). Hearing has long been the primary sense we have addressed in worship, and that is why the nature of our auditory worship is so critical. Are the sounds we use in worship helping people to experience God more fully? This is a direct challenge to those of us who deliver sermons, but it goes beyond preaching to all the ways we communicate through sound. Every word spoken and every sound produced in our worship gatherings has the potential to make a significant impact. It is a question of not only the meaning of those sounds but also their functional clarity and aesthetic quality.

Because music is a purely auditory experience and one of the most established modes of our worship, it is obviously critical that we consider the effectiveness of our music. We all understand that the type of music we use in worship must connect with our culture if we hope to reach out to those around us. However, this is not to say that the music of the church should simply be a pale reflection of the music in the surrounding culture. The church should be the artistic leader of our culture, setting the standard for artistic excellence. Erwin McManus, pastor of the rapidly growing church Mosaic, has recently challenged us to reclaim our role as "cultural architects" in the emerging world.[1] This means that the music of our worship should both engage and transform our culture.

Musical *style* as well as musical *quality* have major impact on the auditory experience in worship. While we value the willingness of every volunteer in our ministry who serves, we also recognize the biblical design of gift-based ministry. Those who lead music in our worship should have the gifts to do so with excellence. The standard will vary based on the size and makeup of each congregation, but as in every area of our ministry, it is essential that the quality of our music in worship is the very best we have to offer.

This is true of our technology and those who run it as well. More and more, the music of our culture is dependent on the quality of the sound system. If we have outdated and inadequate sound technology and untrained people operating it, the auditory experience of worship will be severely compromised. This applies to not only music but also all of the sounds of our worship: preaching, prayer, readings, drama, and so on. We should be investing some of the money we used to spend on pipe organs in the latest sound systems. The size and scope will vary from congregation to congregation, but buy the best equipment your church can afford so that you can use sound in the most effective way possible.

In addition to more structured forms of music, ambient sound can be used to create a certain environment by utilizing various auditory textures. Be aware not only of the impact of sound but the lack of it as well. This is true of how we address all the senses. In our media-obsessed society, people often suffer from sensory overload. Sometimes there is power in addressing the senses through the absence of input. Great musical compositions are marked by frequent rests. Silence can be as meaningful as a beautiful song when we provide quiet space in the cacophony of life and help people learn to listen to God.

SEEING WORSHIP

Visual experience is perhaps the most underutilized aspect of worship in most churches today. Jesus often used visual images when he was teaching. We read his words in the Sermon on the Mount about the birds of the air and the lilies of the field, forgetting that he was speaking on a hillside surrounded by the very lilies and birds of which he spoke! (See Matthew 6:26-30.) In ancient times, Christian worship was a vivid experience through the inclusion of visual arts in worship. One of the oldest places of Christian worship ever discovered intact, the house church of Dura-Europa, has an interior covered with colorful frescoes depicting biblical themes. The churches of the Middle Ages and Renaissance were filled with mosaics, paintings, stained glass, and statuary that all enveloped the worshiper in a visual experience of God. The effort of the Reformers to correct superstition and idolatry resulted in an overcompensation that has left many of our churches visually barren.

In the meantime, our culture has become more and more image-driven. As Leonard Sweet points out, "We are a print-saturated, word-based church in the midst of visual technologies that are creating a whole new visual culture."[2] Images are quickly becoming the primary language of our time, while the church is still speaking a medieval dialect of the printed word. What the printing press did for the written word at the time of the Reformation, the computer, the Internet, digital cameras, and the video projector are doing for images in our time. As you begin to use more visual images in your worship gatherings, you will deepen the experience of worship for your members and become a beacon of hope for countless people in the emerging culture who are looking for a spiritual center in a dislocated world.

If we would spend as much time searching the Internet and other sources for compelling visuals to convey our message as we do for quotes and stories, we would greatly increase our effectiveness in preaching. For the cost of what many churches spend advertising in the religion section of the local paper for a year, you can purchase a video projector that will allow you to add powerful visual impact to your worship. Many churches are already using video projection to display the words of songs and outlines of sermons, but there is tremendous potential for deeper experiences of worship when we move beyond words into the creative use of ancient art, contemporary graphics, artistic photography, and thematic video. During a sermon on the true identity of Jesus, one church projected various paintings from different times and cultures to illustrate how we tend to portray Jesus in our own terms. Another church used a haunting series of black and white photos taken in the inner city set to an evocative sound track during a service focused on our call to serve the outcast and downtrodden. As we learn to utilize creative imagery in all aspects of our worship services, we will reach more and more people in our increasingly visual society.

Even if you can't afford a video projector, pick up a slide projector at a garage sale and recruit some photographers from your congregation; buy fabric and butcher paper and turn your visual artists loose; use ordinary household items to add power to your messages. Give people something meaningful to look at. One church, during a service on finding our place to serve others in the world, had two people on the platform completing a puzzle of the globe, a visual representation of the message. Another friend of mine once placed a recliner on the center of the platform for a service on complacency and invited a worshiper to come have a seat while he described the dangers of getting too comfortable. Having someone gifted in sign language artfully signing worship songs can help the hearing-impaired and give people a beautiful picture of what they are singing. One time, after preaching on the fact that our sins nailed Jesus to the cross, I led a time of confession while holding a large wooden mallet and a long iron spike in my hands. This image struck home more than some of the videos and elaborate visual presentations we have done.

TOUCHING WORSHIP

When you read the Gospels, one of the striking characteristics of Jesus is that he was always touching people—even those who weren't supposed to be touched. It is impossible to overstate the importance of physical touch in reinforcing the more abstract expressions of worship. Think of the inadequacy of telling your children you love them but never hugging them or touching them in loving ways. Clinical studies with newborns have proven that physical touch is necessary to healthy development. However, in a society where child abuse and sexual harassment are tragically common, many have also experienced the destructive power of touch. Because of this, we often find ourselves afraid to touch others, not knowing how that contact might be interpreted. For this very reason, people today are longing for safe, life-giving physical contact. For those who live alone, church may be the only place they can receive meaningful physical contact. If we want to touch their hearts and souls, we will find ways to touch them physically as well.

It is important that we reclaim the power of the tactile in our worship today. How often do you invite people to touch each other during the service? The liturgical practice of "passing the peace" during worship is a continuation of the biblical admonition to "greet one another with a holy kiss" (Romans 16:16). Obviously, this needs to be done in a sensitive way that respects privacy and does not pressure new worshipers into awkward situations. In our culture, asking people to kiss strangers would be counterproductive! However, if passing the peace is not part of your tradition, finding appropriate ways to invite people into positive physical contact during worship will help them experience God. For instance, occasionally we will do something as simple as asking the whole congregation to hold hands while singing the closing song of a service about Christian community. A simple act such as this can be a wonderful way to physically experience the message even though it will pull some people out of their comfort zone.

It is significant that Jesus made it a point to go to John at the Jordan River and be baptized before beginning his ministry (see Mark 1:9). John knew that Jesus didn't need to be baptized, but Jesus insisted. Why? So that by following his example, we would have a way to experience his cleansing and forgiveness through the sense of touch. While Christians will continue to disagree about the precise meaning and mode of baptism, we can all agree that water provides an evocative symbol and tactile experience of God's grace. How often do you give people a chance to reexperience the meaning of their baptism in worship? An example of this is the liturgical practice of providing basins of water in which people can dip their fingers as they enter the worship space. Our church included a flowing water element in the design of our new building to help connect people physically to their baptism. What could you do in your setting to give people a tactile reminder of their baptism?

In the ancient church, laying on of hands and anointing with oil were common ways of using touch to convey the healing and sending power of the Holy Spirit to people. Do you offer the opportunity for this biblical practice on a regular basis? After training volunteer prayer ministers, our church began offering a time in our worship for people to come forward to kneel at a prayer station for personal prayer, the laying on of hands, and the option of anointing. This is not superstition but a biblical practice of engaging the sense of touch in worship, and it can produce powerful moments for those who participate.

TASTING AND SMELLING WORSHIP

It never ceases to amaze me how a scent can evoke meaningful thoughts and memories, and I must admit that the taste of a delicious meal is one of the great joys of my life. Why would we ignore these vital senses in our attempts to help people experience the goodness and power of God? From living in the Holy Land and visiting many ancient churches, I have developed an association between the smell of incense and being in a holy place. One whiff of frankincense takes me right back to those special places and experiences. Psalm 34:8 says, "O taste and see that the LORD is good." Revelation 5:8 describes the offering of pungent incense as a symbol of the prayers of the saints.

By default, people will come to associate a smell with a place. One friend told me that she was always reminded of her childhood church experience by the irritating smell of strong industrial cleaners. Wouldn't it be better if people associated a smell with worship that reinforces the experience instead of takes away from it? Some people are allergic or very sensitive to certain substances, so we need to consider our options with discretion. If incense does not work in your setting, what aroma can you use that will help people experience the holiness of that place? Something as simple as scented candles can create an atmosphere that opens people to God. Sometimes we can use the power of smell to convey a particular message. One Sunday, our church was focusing on Jesus as the Bread of Life, so we set up bread machines all around our worship space. As people entered the gathering, they were greeted by the aroma of freshly baking bread. As we began to explore this biblical teaching, people were not just *thinking* about the Bread of Life; they were truly *experiencing* it.

Jesus went to great lengths to make sure he was able to share the Passover meal with his disciples before he was arrested; he wanted to leave us with a way to experience the power of his forgiving presence through the senses of taste and smell. The way in which Christians should interpret and approach Communion will continue to be debated, but we can all agree that bread and wine (or grape juice) provide a vivid experience of God's presence and grace through the senses of taste and smell. What a wonderful gift Jesus gave us in the Lord's Supper! We not only *hear* that Jesus gave his body and blood for us on the cross but we also *taste* and *smell* the truth of those words when we eat the bread and drink from the cup. As we embrace this gift, those from a less sacramental background will discover how significant Communion can be as a physical experience of worship. Those from a sacramental background may be more familiar with this dynamic but can find creative new ways of celebrating Communion to make the experience fresh and more meaningful. Whatever our background, let's engage all the senses as we invite people into a foretaste of the eternal feast to come.

Chapter 6

CREATING SPACE AND OPPORTUNITY FOR PHYSICAL WORSHIP

WHOLE-BODY EXPERIENCES

Some medieval European churches developed the use of the labyrinth as an expression of physical worship. These ancient Christian labyrinths, often built into the floor of great cathedrals, outlined a complex circular pathway that took the worshiper on a circuitous route into the center and back out again. The worshiper was encouraged to walk the path in a prayerful manner, symbolically acting out the spiritual journey of following Christ.

CLASSICAL LABYRINTH DESIGN

Today Christians of every background are rediscovering the power of this whole-body experience of worship, and labyrinths are popping up everywhere. The symbolism of the historical labyrinth is myriad: the circuitous route reflects the unpredictability of life in a broken world, the journey to the center reminds us of our ever-deepening intimacy with God, and the journey from the center out reminds us of our call to go into the world.[1]

Some have developed new forms of the labyrinth. One approach, renamed "The Prayer Path," still involves walking a pathway, but participants listen to an audio recording on a portable CD player with headphones. The recording guides them through various experiential stations ranging from standing in their bare feet in a box of sand to watching a looping video of waterfalls.[2] During the reflective season of Lent the last several years, our church has set up different "Prayer Paths" to provide a physical spiritual experience. The response has been amazing. Afterward, participants wrote notes to God, such as, "Dear God, what an awesome experience to have this time with you"; "Dear God, I feel I have gotten to know you better mentally, physically, and spiritually. I needed this today, and sharing this with you is an experience I will never forget"; "Dear God, this was a wonderful and amazing experience to focus on your love"; and "Thank you, Father, for meeting me here."[3] Using tape on the floor along the back and side aisles of the worship space, one church group developed a prayer path that worshipers can use during the service itself. Another church group established a prayer path around their campus and invited people to walk it during worship.

What is it about the labyrinth that is so appealing to people in this emerging culture? In the course of my ministry, I have led more than fifty retreats ranging from two days to two weeks in length. Over and over again, I have seen the life-changing impact of placing yourself in a new environment: we see things from a different point of view, the sounds and sights and smells are different, and we open ourselves to a new way of experiencing God. None of our senses operate in isolation, but each is interconnected to the others. For this reason, it is important to consider the role of what I call "whole-body experiences" in our worship gatherings. A whole-body experience is one in which people engage all of their senses at once by putting their bodies into different environments.

Whenever people get up out of their seats and do something, they are having complete sensory experiences. How often do people get up and move to a different place during your worship gatherings? Typically people come into a worship service, sit down, and do not move from that spot until the service is over. Often the physical limitations of our space contribute to this: fixed seating, not enough room for people to move around, and so on. In spite of this, it is important to find ways to allow people to get up and change their environment during worship.

The Roman Catholic Eucharist, Southern Baptist altar calls, and Brethren foot washings are traditional examples of whole-body experiences. If your worship space allows, it can be effective to create specific places where people can engage in some significant activity as a part of the worship experience. During some services, our church offers five different "experiential stations." We set aside twenty minutes of singing during which people are free to visit any or all of the stations in order to have a whole-body experience of worship. In other services, to support a particular theme, we invite people to come forward and participate in a symbolic act, such as lighting a candle, dropping a rock into a bowl of water, laying a written confession at the foot of the cross, drawing on a butcher-paper mural on the wall, or hanging a leaf on a barren tree.

On All Saints' Day, one church focused on the inspiring example of those who have gone before us in the faith. Near the end of the service, they invited people to come forward and light a candle in memory of someone who had passed away and was an example of faith. It was a compelling moment for their whole community as people came forward with tears streaming down their faces. Whole-body experiences can be this simple or more complex, as long as they convey a symbolic meaning. During a service centered on Jesus' reinstatement of Peter after his denial, people wrote down their failures to God. We had positioned electric paper shredders along the front of our worship space, and as people came forward to receive Communion, they were invited to shred their papers as an act of absolution. The sound of those failures being ground up and spit out communicated forgiveness in a surprisingly fresh way! At one Maundy Thursday service at our church, the congregation was invited to come forward and take a piece of bread for Communion directly from loaves affixed to a large rustic cross at the center of the platform. The next night, at our Good Friday service, people came forward and dripped red wax on the same cross, which held the torn remnants of bread from the night before. This experience brought home the sacrifice of Jesus and what it means to us in a way that staying seated in a chair never could.

As in other aspects of public life, those who are able-bodied are called to consider the needs of the physically challenged. When planning whole-body experiences, do whatever you can to make them accessible to as many people as possible. Consider how the experience can be brought to people in their seats if necessary. Ask God to help your creative team produce opportunities for all people to participate in acts of worship that involve their whole bodies, drawing them into more complete encounters with God, which in turn will change their lives.

SPACE MATTERS

I love church buildings and have always been a fan of great architecture. All my life, I have loved walking into various kinds of worship spaces and experiencing the impact of each place. From the grandeur of a Gothic cathedral to the simplicity of a Quaker meetinghouse, the space in which we worship has an impact on the nature of the experience. The cathedral draws us into the transcendence of God, while the meetinghouse draws us into the fellowship of the community. Every kind of ecclesiastical architecture reflects something about the values and focus of a particular tradition and culture. There is a fellowship I have attended that meets in a casino bar. Another church near mine meets in a huge sports arena. These settings impact the experience of these congregations and say something about their purposes.

Imagine walking into a crowded nightclub: loud music, low lights, the crush of the crowd, the pulsating energy of the dance floor. Now imagine walking into the large library of a prestigious university: silence, open space, rows of books, privacy. Just walking into those two different spaces evokes radically different experiences. Each place facilitates a different kind of activity. Imagine trying to study chemistry in the nightclub or meeting with your friends for an evening out at the library. Environments create feelings, stimulate thoughts, and trigger responses. A brightly lit room with lots of windows creates a different mood than a candlelit room shrouded with drapes.

It has been said that we shape our worship space and then our worship space shapes us. From the time people enter the place where you are holding worship, the ambient characteristics of that space will affect their experience. There are pros and cons to every kind of physical setting. Each of us has a worship space that works for or against our purposes to some degree at any given time. The size and shape of the room, its configuration, the furniture, the lighting, the temperature, the colors, and even the texture of the surfaces all impact the experience of worshiping in that place.

A few years ago, our church had the privilege and challenge of building a brand new worship center. We sought to design a space that not only reflected our aesthetics and tradition, but also, more important, allowed us to facilitate worship that is highly experiential.

The design had lots of nice windows, but these made video projection and dramatic lighting nearly impossible. So we added retractable shades that let us control the lighting, maximize our two rear-projection video screens, and create various moods. By utilizing a wide and shallow layout, we were able to double our seating capacity but create an environment that felt twice as intimate as our old long, narrow layout. We kept the platform area open and flexible to allow for every kind of configuration. We made sure the building utilized the most current technology we could afford and allowed for future adaptation as technology changes. Our worship center has a very contemporary feel to match our cultural context, but we also wanted to create a visual connection to the ancient roots of our biblical faith. A gifted designer and wood-carver helped us incorporate a large central cross and beautifully carved elements based on the imagery of Revelation 22, the tree of life and the river of life.[4] Although much of our worship is very contemporary in style, we wanted to be able to utilize traditional postures of worship, such as kneeling, in all our services, so we included kneelers in the seating design.

Most of us don't have the luxury of designing our physical worship space. We have to deal with what we have. But there are many things you can do to facilitate a more experiential environment for worship. First, reexamine your worship space with the eye of a first-time visitor. What is the visual impact? What kind of feeling does the environment evoke? Does the space work for or against the goals of Experiential Worship? What are the things you can change? What things can't be changed? How can you maximize the potential of the parts you can't change? What are the most important changes that you can afford? How can you increase the flexibility of the space?

One of the key factors in creating an Experiential Worship environment is lighting. Most churches don't have enough lighting and overuse what they do have. It's critical to be able to control the lights to provide clear visibility for those leading from the front and still create low lighting or even darkness where people are sitting, which can facilitate a feeling of mystery and privacy.

Colors evoke different feelings. Consider the environment you want to create, and pick paint accordingly. What about the seating arrangement? Is there any way to reconfigure seating so people are more connected to those who are leading and to each other? The use of technology is also critical. How can you provide vivid visual images for the whole congregation? Is there enough floor space to allow people to actively participate in experiential opportunities? If not, how can you make room for this?

In our ministry, a major discovery was the power of ambient arts. It is amazing the impact a piece of cloth, artfully hung with a particular purpose, can have on the feeling of your worship space. We have teams of volunteers gifted in interior design and decoration who shape the feeling of our worship space by creating unique decorations and displays for certain seasons or worship series. Often during Lent they hang large swaths of purple cloth from the ceiling and then overlay a huge crown of thorns for a powerful visual impact. Once, during a series on spiritual renewal, they created a desolate garden that sprouted colorful flowers each week until, by the end of the series, the garden was bursting with new life. Though their budget is small, through ingenuity and hard work they help create a more experiential environment. Rather than thinking of your physical space as a static building that confines your worship, think of it as a canvas upon which your members can use their gifts to create a setting more conducive to encountering God.

Beyond Multisensory Worship

We have only scratched the surface of the possibilities for engaging all the physical senses in worship. In this discussion, I have offered concrete examples in the hope they will stimulate the creativity of your community and motivate you to seek the Spirit's guidance in discovering unique ways to engage people through their senses in your context. In part 6, I suggest ideas for a process by which you can begin to plan, implement, and lead Experiential Worship on a regular basis, but this too is meant to inspire you to design a process that works in your setting.

The mistake we often make in talking about multisensory worship is to get so enamored with the techniques and ideas that we forget that the point of addressing the senses is to create a transforming experience. Dan Kimball says, "We can easily get caught up in trying new worship tricks and cool innovative things in worship . . . [but this] reduces us to performers and reduces church attendees to mere judges."[5] The value of every idea and approach is measured by its effectiveness in conveying an experience of God and facilitating authentic worship rather than how trendy or "cool" it is. Focusing primarily on the creative forms rather than the God we serve will create a consumer culture that contradicts the very nature of worship itself.

The reason physical aspects of worship are important is that they point us to deeper realities. Visible acts of worship are always intended to connect us to the invisible reality of God. We make a fatal mistake if we think the physical act itself is worship. The biblical distinction between Creator and creation is critical. Failure to make this distinction puts us in danger of idolatry or at least reducing worship to "going through the motions." When we identify authentic worship with a particular external act, we also become prone to legalistic attitudes and self-serving pride, which is the very opposite of the worship we are trying to facilitate.

Every Christian community is made up of a unique combination of leadership, tradition, gifts, vision, context, and resources. For that reason, every congregation is called to find new ways to create worship gatherings that engage the whole person. What we are doing in my church will vary from what you do in yours because we have different leaders, come from divergent backgrounds, have variously gifted members, have a unique God-given vision for our ministry, are placed in a specific cultural setting, and have different resources available to us. As we learn from each other and draw from a broader range of Christian traditions, the Holy Spirit will show us unique ways to manifest life-changing worship in our time and place.

Part Three

MindWorship:
Engaging and Transforming the Intellect

*Do not be conformed to this world, but be transformed
by the renewing of your minds.*
Romans 12:2

Chapter 7

COMPREHENDING THE INCOMPREHENSIBLE

FROM UNKNOWN TO KNOWN

Athens, the ancient headquarters of wisdom and learning, had formed the foundations of Western civilization. Paul felt a long way from Tarsus, where the temples and monuments of his hometown were modeled after the architecture of this great city. The age-old Parthenon, perched atop the Acropolis and casting its imposing shadow over this birthplace of Greek philosophy, appeared to challenge even the grandeur of Jerusalem, with its towering Temple Mount. As he walked through the Agora at the city's center, Paul's agile mind was buzzing with thoughts sparked by the sights surrounding him. In every direction stood a different temple to yet another god of the Greek and Roman pantheon. A strong passion rose inside of him as he gazed upon this orgy of idolatry, aware of his growing desire to unfetter minds that had been deceived by myth and human invention.

Day after day, Paul had addressed the leaders of the Athenian synagogue, showing from the Scriptures that Jesus is the long-awaited Messiah, but he was shocked by their unwillingness to even consider what he had to say. Perhaps their minds had been hardened in the face of the pagan philosophy they had to confront every day in this most intellectual of cities. Even Paul's attempts to proclaim the good news in the Athenian marketplace had been an uphill battle. The Epicurean and Stoic philosophers that he met there seemed unable to comprehend what Paul kept trying so hard to explain. Gradually, he began to realize that once and for all their whole frame of reference was so different that he could no longer rely on his familiar strategy of quoting the Hebrew prophets and referring to the Law of Moses to make a case for Jesus' divinity. How was he supposed to teach the efficacy of the cross when concepts such as substitutional atonement and propitiation for sin were foreign to them? He knew he needed a different approach.

Passing by an altar labeled, "To an unknown god," Paul allowed himself a wry smile. "Covering all their bases," he thought to himself and then mused on the irony of so much wisdom and religion yet so little knowledge of the true God. Suddenly it hit him: *This is the approach I've been looking for.* His pulse quickened as he began to ascend the hill of the Areopagus. One of the Epicureans had invited him to address the famous philosophical council of Athens—an unprecedented opportunity to proclaim the gospel to the leading thinkers of the city.

Looking out over the learned faces of the council, Paul took a deep breath and began: "Athenians, I see how extremely religious you are in every way, for as I went through the city and looked carefully at the objects of your worship, I found among them an altar with the inscription 'To an unknown god.' What therefore you worship as unknown, this I proclaim to you." The words were beginning to flow, and Paul felt his strength building as he went on to describe the holiness and compassion of the God whom they had for so long only known in vague shadows and heard in distant echoes. He threw in a couple of quotes from the Greek poets he had read, and he saw a flash of recognition pass over some faces. After pointing out the futility of idol worship, Paul concluded by calling for repentance and inviting the Athenians to put their trust in the Jesus who conquered death through his resurrection.

Paul was used to the reactions that came when he proclaimed the Resurrection, a stumbling block to Jews and folly to Gentiles. Some of the council openly scoffed at the claim that Jesus had risen from the dead. "Nonsense!" "Impossible!" But others were intrigued by the compelling logic of Paul's argument and invited him to return the next day for more discussion. As he was getting ready to leave, a man named Dionysius, a member of the Areopagus, silently approached Paul and pulled him into

a private corner. In conspiratorial tones, he confided to Paul that he had
always sought the unknown god because he sensed there must be more
than the Greek myths he had grown up with. He told Paul in a whisper,
"When you were speaking, it suddenly became clear to me. I believe what
you said is true and I want to find out how to become a follower of this
Jesus." Thrilled, Paul invited him to join the other believers in Athens for a
time of worship and made arrangements to meet with him afterward to talk
more about his fledgling faith. (adapted from Acts 17:16-34)

COMPREHENDING GOD

From the beginning of human memory, people have searched for their
Creator. Intrigued by the mystery, they have reached out for the unknown
God, constructing myths and religions to fill the void. Noble as these human
attempts were, it was only when God broke the silence and spoke to people
like Noah and Abraham and Moses that the impenetrable shroud was pulled
back by divine revelation. No longer was God a distant concept, shaped
by imagination, superstition, and extrapolation. Now God spoke directly,
clearly: "I have set my bow in the clouds," "I will make of you a great
nation," "I AM WHO I AM" (Genesis 9:13; 12:2; Exodus 3:14). These revelatory
moments were more the exception than the rule, but they formed markers
on the path to a limited human comprehension of God.

The Hebrew Scriptures chronicle the initiative of God revealing himself to
humanity through words, recorded and passed down through the centuries.
Powerful and illuminating as they were, somehow these words of divine
self-disclosure were not enough, so God took the next step. John opens his
gospel, "In the beginning was the Word, and the Word was with God, and
the Word was God. . . . And the Word became flesh and lived among us,
and we have seen his glory, the glory as of a father's only son, full of grace
and truth" (John 1:1,14).

The miracle of the Word is that the transcendent God of the universe
chose to become immanent by expressing himself in human language and
as a human being. John used the Greek term *logos*, laden with philosophical
inference, to capture the truth that we have a God who not only speaks but
also makes himself comprehensible to the human intellect. God has chosen

to express himself in a rational, reasonable way so that we might come to know and understand him with our minds.

God far exceeds our ability to comprehend him. As Paul says, "For God's foolishness is wiser than human wisdom, and God's weakness is stronger than human strength" (1 Corinthians 1:25). Yet God has decided to squeeze himself into human language and the person of Jesus Christ so that as we "search for God and perhaps grope for him" we might be able to find him (Acts 17:27). In the written Word of Scripture and the living Word of Jesus, God has measured out a thimble-sized portion of himself that our cups might be filled to overflowing with his grace and truth. The good news that Paul so effectively proclaimed to the Athenian philosophers is that the "unknown god" has become for us the God who can be known even through our finite human intellect!

REASONABLE WORSHIP

Have you ever put your foot in your mouth only to remember the old saying "Do not operate mouth until brain is engaged"? Operating the body without engaging the mind can be a dangerous thing. Have you ever arrived at home and not been able to remember actually driving there? Scary, huh? To invite people into acts of worship without engaging their minds is equally hazardous. Ultimately, it doesn't matter what we are saying or doing in worship if we don't know what it means. You've probably heard of the little boy who began the Lord's Prayer, "Our Father, who art in heaven, Harold be thy name." Another kindergartner continued, "Give us this day our jelly bread." One little girl prayed, "Forgive us our dentists, as we forgive our dentists." Another boy pleaded, "Lead us not into creation," followed by the farmer's son, who said, "And deliver us from weevils." A media-savvy little girl triumphantly concluded, "For thine is the kingdom and the power and the glory, forever and ever. Amen and FM." When we don't know the meaning of the words we are speaking, we can end up saying almost anything.

It should be no surprise that Jesus called us to love God with all of our minds. God is not interested in mindless worship. If people are not engaged intellectually, anything else that we do will be meaningless, for the mind is where we register the meaning of our actions. Paul explained this to the

Corinthians when they were overemphasizing the gift of tongues in worship: "For if I pray in a tongue, my spirit prays but my mind is unproductive. What should I do then? I will pray with the spirit, but I will pray with the mind also; I will sing praise with the spirit, but I will sing praise with the mind also" (1 Corinthians 14:14-15).

In Romans 12:1, Paul described authentic worship this way: "I appeal to you therefore, brothers and sisters, by the mercies of God, to present your bodies as a living sacrifice, holy and acceptable to God, which is your spiritual worship." The word *body* in this context refers not only to our physical selves but also to *all* that we are, hearts, souls, minds, and bodies. True worship is offering our whole selves to God in response to his infinite mercies toward us. Paul describes this as our "spiritual worship." The root of the Greek word translated "spiritual" here is *logos*. Another way to translate this word is "reasonable." Paul is telling us that "spiritual" worship engages the whole person and is comprehendible according to human reason. To emphasize this, he goes on in the very next verse to say, "Do not be conformed to this world, but be transformed by the renewing of your minds, so that you may discern what is the will of God—what is good and acceptable and perfect."

When our minds are engaged in this kind of "reasonable" worship, we learn to discern God's will for our lives, our minds are renewed so we begin to think differently, and our whole selves enter into a process of transformation. Experiential Worship is always reasonable worship so that it can transform the minds of those who experience it.

MINDING OUR WORSHIP

I once attended a worship service of a large, growing congregation. The facilities were state of the art, the logistics of the service were well organized, and the music was excellent. I laughed at the drama. I was moved by a story. I felt good as I was clapping and singing upbeat songs. As my family and I drove away, I was remarking what a great service it was, when it suddenly hit me that I could not say what the service had actually been about. I could describe the various elements of the service, but I could not identify the meaning of those elements. While I had offered my genuine praise to God,

I had not learned anything new. There was no biblical insight that set me free in some way. I was not any more equipped to follow Jesus because of attending the service. This worship experience had engaged my body and, to some extent, my emotions but not my mind. When trying to develop culturally relevant worship, there is a dangerous tendency to substitute creativity and innovation for solid biblical content.

How can we offer worship experiences that engage people intellectually and have a lasting effect on their lives? Only by making relevant biblical content the core and foundation of every worship gathering. We can offer the most effective multisensory service that leads people into a powerful emotional experience, but if there is not solid biblical content conveyed to the mind, then our labor is in vain. The writer of Hebrews rebukes his readers for becoming "dull in understanding" (5:11) and then diagnoses the problem this way: "For everyone who lives on milk, being still an infant, is unskilled in the word of righteousness. But solid food is for the mature" (5:13-14).

If our worship services offer only milk, we shouldn't be surprised that many of our members are not maturing in their faith. If we do not also feed them meat, we cannot expect them to develop as followers of Jesus. A varied and balanced diet in worship will develop strong disciples. Experiential Worship provides milk for the newcomer by ensuring that every service is understandable and inviting to seekers but at the same time offers solid food that engages the minds of believers and challenges them to deeper thinking about God's Word and a clearer understanding of their faith. To err on either end of this spectrum is to exclude newcomers or consign our members to spiritual malnutrition.

What determines the core content of your services? Is it the perceived needs of your congregation? Is it the current issues important in your community? Is it a predetermined denominational program? Is it an historical liturgical format? All of these factors can be significant, but none is sufficient. Worship that transforms the mind always begins with the Word of God. It is the truth of the Bible, centered on the person of Jesus, that provides the balanced diet that will renew the minds of our worshipers in our churches and transform their lives.

Chapter 8

FROM TRUTH TO UNDERSTANDING

CONNECTING MINDS

On the very first evening of our trip through Europe, my sister, Leslie, and I drove into the West German town of Bayreuth in our VW Beetle. For the first time in our young lives, we were faced with the daunting task of survival. If we did not find a place to stay, we would not have a bed that night. If we did not find a place to eat, we would not have dinner that night. Our initial attempts to find the local youth hostel were unsuccessful, so Leslie finally convinced me to ask directions from a pedestrian. I rolled down the window and, in a well-rehearsed German phrase, asked for directions. The man on the sidewalk assumed I could actually speak German and proceeded to let forth a torrent of guttural Germanic sounds unlike anything I had ever heard. I nodded, smiled, and rolled up the window as we drove away. After a moment of silence, Leslie asked, "Well, what did he say?" I turned to her and sheepishly admitted, "I have no idea."

I am positive the man on the sidewalk gave me directions that were accurate. It was important information that I sorely needed, and he acted in good faith, intending to help me find my way. The only problem was that the information did not make it from him to me. Too often, this is what happens to people in our worship gatherings. With great enthusiasm, we proclaim thoughts, ideas, and information that people desperately need, but rather than finding direction through the confusing maze of life, they simply nod, smile, and drive away. Even if we're accurately proclaiming God's Word, it does them no good if the truth never reaches them intellectually.

What is it that keeps the worshipers in our services from understanding and receiving the transforming truth of God's Word that we proclaim? To begin with, we are sharing a story that took place two to three thousand years ago on the other side of the planet in a completely different kind of culture. On top of that, the story was written down in vastly different languages that don't even share our Western alphabet and have been translated into English at various times by different people. As if these hurdles weren't enough, most of our churches are caught in a parochial time warp. We use a technical vocabulary few people understand, we assume a background of knowledge even fewer possess, and we utilize modes of communication most people can't relate to. No wonder our message sounds incomprehensible to the ears of most unchurched people today!

A hundred years ago, the primary mode of communication was the spoken word. The principal form of entertainment was being read to. The familiar form of music was choral singing. It makes sense that these would make up the primary forms of worship in the churches of those times. People were used to sitting and listening to long orations with complex literary allusions. People loved to sing hymns led by a choir and organ or piano. Today we live in a vastly changed world. Ours is a media-saturated, technologically driven, visual culture. Many people don't read books anymore; they surf the Web and watch movies. Most people are not used to listening to long speeches; they catch sound bites and look at graphics that portray information visually. Few people today listen to choral music except when they come to church.

It should not surprise us that when we give long speeches and follow up with choral singing, our people are unmoved. We are speaking a cultural language that most people do not understand. Engaging the mind in reasonable worship begins with the Word of God, but it requires us to seek more effective ways to communicate that biblical content throughout the worship experience.

Jesus' Mind Language

Imagine sitting on a hillside overlooking a sparkling blue lake, watching the long grass sway back and forth to the music of the wind. You breathe deeply and smile as the morning breeze serves up the delicious scent of blooming lilies. You hear the birds calling out their simple songs as they dart back and forth overhead. It is good to be here, but you can't help worrying. After all, you had to leave your fields untended to come hear this controversial Galilean rabbi teach. Laboring under the weight of Roman taxation, it takes every ounce of effort just to get by these days. Looking at your children's tattered clothes, you wonder how you will keep them warm and well fed this winter. Then Jesus' piercing voice cuts through your anxious thoughts:

> "Therefore I tell you, do not worry about your life, what you will eat or what you will drink, or about your body, what you will wear. Is not life more than food, and the body more than clothing? Look at the birds of the air; they neither sow nor reap nor gather into barns, and yet your heavenly Father feeds them. Are you not of more value than they? And can any of you by worrying add a single hour to your span of life? And why do you worry about clothing? Consider the lilies of the field, how they grow; they neither toil nor spin, yet I tell you, even Solomon in all his glory was not clothed like one of these. But if God so clothes the grass of the field, which is alive today and tomorrow is thrown into the oven, will he not much more clothe you—you of little faith? Therefore do not worry, saying, 'What will we eat?' or 'What will we drink?' or 'What will we wear?' For it is the Gentiles who strive for all these things; and indeed your heavenly Father knows that you need all these things. But strive first for the kingdom of God and his righteousness, and all these things will be given to you as well." (Matthew 6:25-33)

Jesus effectively combined divine insight with culturally relevant modes of communication. He drew on the experiences of his listeners to make this truth come alive for them. He understood the pressures of subsistence-level farmers laboring under the weight of oppressive taxation. He spoke to that need, drawing on the sights, smells, and sounds that surrounded them. He employed metaphors woven into the fabric of their lives, such as sowing and reaping. He used object lessons based on realities they had seen operating all their lives, such as the subsistence of birds and the beauty of lilies. His call to trust God rather than to worry had power, not only because it was true but also because Jesus communicated it to people in a way they could grasp.

The emerging culture of our time is becoming more and more like the culture in which Jesus taught—a world of symbols, stories, and concrete images rather than of abstract rational discourse. The time has come for us to return to the communication methods of Jesus and apply them in ways that are relevant to people in our time and place. If we hope to engage people intellectually with the life-changing truth of the Word, we will need to reclaim metaphor, simile, parable, story, object lesson, and visual reinforcement in our communication.

People in the emerging culture are increasingly shaped by imaginative, experience-based forms of communication. While most of us who plan and lead worship have been trained in the doctrines of modern communication, the language of our time is no longer conceptual but metaphorical. As we develop a more metaphorical vocabulary, we will communicate more effectively and engage people's minds more fully.

Chapter 9

STRATEGIES TO CONNECT WITH THE MIND

METAPHORS AND THE MIND

Metaphors are concrete images that carry one or more symbolic meanings. Words are used to paint pictures in people's minds that vividly convey ideas. Jesus was a master at evoking whole worlds of meaning through words like "salt," "lampstand," "gate," and "wolves" (Matthew 5:13,15; 7:13,15). When Jesus called the Pharisees "whitewashed tombs" (Matthew 23:27), he made a vivid point through that one metaphorical phrase. Jesus also developed more complex, overarching metaphors, such as "the kingdom of God," that tied together many truths in his teaching. Developing worship that engages the mind involves learning to use the whole range of metaphor in our communication as Jesus did.

In my church, we try to have at least one central metaphor that runs through every series and each service. We look for metaphors that are vivid and meaningful to members of our church and unchurched newcomers alike. We use them to communicate the biblical truth we are focusing on in that particular series or worship gathering. If these metaphors are unfamiliar to the worshipers or can't be clearly connected to the biblical message, they will not be effective. The best metaphors are taken from popular culture and have a direct application to biblical truths.

Our church once did a series called "The Fellowship of the Mat,"[1] focusing on our call to team ministry. We utilized the central metaphor of a quest. We drew on the popularity of the newly released *The Lord of the Rings* movie trilogy and the fellowship of creatures from Middle Earth, who were called to go together on a quest to destroy the great and all-powerful Ring. We tied this concept to the biblical example of the four friends who carried their paralyzed friend on a mat to be healed by Jesus in Capernaum, lowering him through the roof. Their quest was to get their friend into the presence of Jesus so he could be healed. We applied this to our calling to come together in ministry teams to carry out God's purposes in the world.

Our visual arts team created a display in the front of our worship space that depicted a cloth mat being lowered through a roof on four ropes. This became the visual representation of the mat as a metaphor for our calling to come together with a group of people around a common kingdom purpose. Each week, we focused on a different characteristic of the four friends in Capernaum and illustrated the nature of team ministry with a different clip from the film *The Fellowship of the Ring*. We capitalized on different aspects of our central metaphor to teach the biblical concept of team ministry.

This is just one example of how we can find an effective metaphor, express it in terms of popular culture, connect it to biblical truth, and apply it to people's lives so that they truly "get" the message we are trying to convey. I find that what people tend to remember about a service or a series is the metaphor, and this connects them to the message. Sometimes these metaphors can take on a life of their own and continue to have lasting meaning in a given community. One church did a series utilizing a plumbing metaphor. The pastor contrasted the function of a bucket (hoarding) with that of a pipe (sharing) and asked people to consider the question "Are you a bucket or a pipe?" Long after the series was over, a simple reference to "plumbing theology" would immediately bring back all the vivid lessons learned during those services.

STORIES AND THE MIND

Jesus loved to tell stories in order to engage people's minds. Matthew tells us, "Jesus told the crowds all these things in parables; without a parable he told them nothing" (Matthew 13:34). Jesus' parables were rooted in real life.

When people listened to Jesus' parables, they could relate to the people and events in the story. The unspoken cultural inferences were as significant as the words.

Stories have the power to engage people's minds and open them to vivid understandings of new truths. In his masterfully written book *Windows of the Soul*, Ken Gire explains, "Stories give us eyes other than our own with which to see the world."[2] He quotes Arthur Gordon: "What the storyteller is doing, of course, is looking through the windows of his imagination, trying to see things more clearly, hoping to help and enlighten, and entertain others at the same time. And sometimes, if the panes in the window are clear, he does."[3] In my congregation, when people make reference to things they remember from a particular worship experience, most often they refer to a story.

If we can recover the art of storytelling, we will effectively engage people on an intellectual level. When we describe a spiritual truth in an abstract way, disconnected from real life, it can seem distant, bland, and impotent to many people. The younger generations are honest enough to tell us the painful truth, "That's boring!" On the day of his graduation from Bible college, a friend said to me, "No one has the right to make the gospel boring!" The message of the Bible is intrinsically exciting, fascinating, and memorable. If our expression of that life-changing message is bland, forgettable, or uninspiring, we are robbing the gospel of its power and failing to help people love God with all their minds.

When we recount a personal story in which we experienced a spiritual truth, people sit up and listen—and they "get it"! When we use the stories of others or fictional stories, we allow people to experience things they otherwise never could. When we invite members of our churches to stand up and tell their stories, we offer people a living parable. When we show videotaped interviews of people sharing different aspects of their lives, we are exposing worshipers to insightful stories. When we read and show children's stories, we are speaking not only to the children present but also to that child who lives inside of every adult. There is no substitute for the power of stories to engage and transform people's minds.

IMAGES AND THE MIND

In addition to utilizing metaphors and stories, Jesus was a visual teacher. When the disciples were admiring the massive stones of the temple, he taught them about the temporal nature of this world and the coming of the next (see Mark 13:1-2). When asked about paying Roman taxes, he directed people's attention to the image of Caesar on a coin (see Mark 12:16). When challenged by the Pharisees on his authority to forgive sins, he invited a paralytic to stand (see Mark 2:9-12). Jesus used the visual backdrop of his "classroom" to make his teaching come alive for the listeners. He was interested in reaching ordinary folks, so he spoke in word pictures, giving people specific visual images to engage their minds with the truth.

Long after the time of Jesus' teaching ministry, researchers have shown that we don't all use the same learning styles. Our educational system has focused on those who learn best by listening to information or reading the printed word, while those who process information most effectively by seeing things or doing things have been overlooked. Enlightened educators have been developing strategies to teach visual and tactile-kinesthetic learners as well as auditory learners. If this is happening in our schools, how much more should we in the church be intentionally developing strategies to intellectually reach people of all different learning styles, especially since Jesus already showed us the way?

Verbal images can be powerful communicators, for the human imagination can conjure up things more fantastic than any special-effects studio. However, people's imaginations need encouragement. When we provide literal visual images to augment our various forms of communication, we help people open their minds and unleash the power of their imaginations. Studies are unanimous on this point. When people see what we are talking about, they will understand more clearly and remember more accurately.

Chapter 10

TOOLS TO CONNECT WITH THE MIND

VISUAL WORSHIP

In our church, we make visual communication an important part of every worship service. First of all, for each worship series, we try to come up with a compelling visual logo that captures the central idea of the series and then use it on program covers, PowerPoint slides, handouts, and any other place we can think of. This helps people focus on the central metaphor of the series and remember where we are going with it. For a series on spiritual gifts titled "Finding Your Fit," we used the image of puzzle pieces fitting together. We did a series titled "Go Against the Flow" on the countercultural message of the prophets. It featured a drawing of a Christian fish swimming in the opposite direction of a sea full of frightening-looking creatures. Just as a corporate logo can evoke memories of your experiences with certain services or products, these kinds of images can bring to mind the theme of a whole worship series.

Our planning team tries to make every worship gathering a visual experience. From the use of color or symbolism to historical art to specially created visual displays to the use of video to high-tech computer-generated presentations, our hope is that people will be able to see what we are communicating so they will understand and receive the message. One Easter we used as a visual focal point the popular painting by Thomas Blackshear titled *Forgiven*. The painting depicts the risen Christ standing behind a contemporary man whose knees are dirty and worn and who is holding a mallet and spike in his hands. The man is collapsing in sorrow, but Jesus has extended his nail-pierced hands to catch the man and lift him up. The background is dark and foreboding, but there is a circle of light emanating from Jesus. There is a small red stream flowing from beneath Jesus' feet, and blooming Easter lilies are growing out of the barren ground.[1]

The Easter message that day emphasized the power of the Resurrection to make the atonement of the cross effective in our lives today. As they left, we gave the worshipers a card with the Blackshear painting on the front and an invitation inside to return for a series based on the painting. On the Sundays that followed, we shared the message of the gospel from consecutive chapters in Romans and drew on a different part of the painting each week. The mallet and spike depicted our guilt, the man's body language represented repentance, the arms of Jesus holding the man depicted God's grace, and so on. This beautiful artwork became a visual parable that communicated the message of salvation in images. I would bet that nearly everyone who attended those services can look at that painting today and tell you the basic message of the gospel because it was made visual for them. One church designed a series around Rembrandt's incredible painting *The Return of the Prodigal Son* to heighten the impact of that parable. A worshiper commented, "It was amazing how much that painting helped me understand the story of the prodigal."

ELECTRONIC IMAGERY

In part 2, I described the power of engaging people visually in worship through the use of video projection, and it is so effective that I want to reiterate it here. Jesus was not afraid to use innovative means to increase the impact of his communication. Remember when he stood in a boat to teach the crowds in Galilee (see Matthew 13:2)? This not only kept the crowd from overwhelming him but it also enabled his voice to carry across the water to a much larger group than he otherwise would have been able to address. The Reformation was largely driven by the power of a new technology, the printing press, to disseminate ideas and information far faster and more cheaply than ever before possible. Today the explosion of the Internet, along with the development of computers and video projection, has the same revolutionary potential.

For every service in my church, we search for evocative images to project that will support and reinforce what we are trying to communicate. Sometimes we utilize electronic images of great historical art to convey the timeless nature of the message. Other times we use insightful photography that captures aspects of reality easily overlooked in real-time experience. Sometimes we project graphic art or simple diagrams that underscore ideas we are helping people to understand. Other times we simply show pictures of things we are describing or locations of stories we are telling. The cumulative effect of these images is that people understand more completely, experience more deeply, and retain more accurately the transforming truth we want to convey.

Sometimes we have an image or looping video on the screens to set a tone as people are entering the worship space or as a backdrop during other elements of a service. Often we use still and moving images alongside or behind the lyrics of worship songs. Sometimes the images appear on the screens without comment as the speaker is talking. When we are using a more complex visual image to help communicate a truth, usually the speaker will refer directly to the image and explain it if necessary. When quoting an individual from popular culture, why not use a picture of him or her while you read the statement? When referring to a recent event, you could show a compelling photo of it from a news website. When describing a scientific fact, try using a chart that illustrates the idea you are hoping to convey.

Because it is made up of almost innumerable different images, video is the most visually intensive way to communicate. We use secular film clips regularly to make memorable visual impressions (see chapter 14 for more on this). There are also many excellent biblical films that can be used to illustrate various narrative texts. THE VISUAL BIBLE series uses biblical text as its script so it can be used in place of a Scripture reading.[2] Some Christian production companies are producing excellent conceptual videos that can be used very effectively. One day we were focusing on marriage and showed a music video in which a man who has been unfaithful to his wife recognizes the mistake he has made and repents, and his wife forgives him to begin the process of healing. Because it came in the context of biblical teaching on marriage, the video created a poignant four minutes that could never have been achieved by simply describing the effects of adultery.

Some churches often use a clip from a documentary that vividly explains important facts relevant to the theme for that day. During a series on Psalm 23, one church showed a segment on how shepherds care for their flocks. Another church used a documentary on mountain climbing to introduce that metaphor for a series on small groups. We once showed part of a documentary on the formation of natural wonders to explain how God can use our struggles to shape us in his image. If pictures speak thousands of words, imagine what an informative video can convey!

As technology develops, there will be more and more resources for using video in creative ways. Online you can find sources for stock video footage of almost anything you can imagine, and with the right presentation software, you can run video loops, animated graphics, or ambient images behind your song lyrics.[3] However, you do not have to rely on professionally produced video to make an impact with this technology. With nothing more than a handheld video camera and a willing volunteer, you can do on-the-street interviews, feature congregation members who would never agree to get up and speak in church, show clips of local events, or create symbolic video collages. Members of a volunteer video ministry team can learn to edit and create their own customized video productions.

LOW-TECH VISUALS

I am convinced that an effective projection system is becoming as important as a good sound system for congregations that want to communicate to our emerging culture. However, even if you decide that electronic image projection does not fit your setting or is currently out of your reach, there are myriad low-tech ways to use visuals to connect more effectively with people's minds. One time, we were doing a worship series based on Max Lucado's book *Traveling Light.* The focus was on learning to let go of unnecessary burdens, and the central metaphor was the experience of traveling with too much baggage. At the front of the worship space, our visual arts team artistically created a huge pile of antique luggage. The bags were labeled with various burdens, such as "fear," "stress," and "guilt." Each week as we dealt with a particular topic, that labeled piece of luggage would be removed, and there was a visual sense that our collective burdens were being lightened by the power of God's Word. Another time, during a series on roadblocks to spiritual growth, we borrowed some orange and white construction barriers and set them up around the platform. Yet another series focused on the image from the book of Revelation of casting our crowns down before the throne of God. We gathered all the trophies we could find and made a kind of sculpture on the platform that became a visual expression of offering all our accomplishments to God as an act of worship.

Some congregations are blessed with people who can do visual art as an act of worship. These uniquely gifted individuals can paint or draw or sculpt during the service and provide a dynamic visual image without using video. If you are not blessed with artists who can do this during the service, nearly every size congregation has people who are gifted to create visual art in other settings that can support the message in worship. In preparation for a series on becoming more like Jesus, a member of our congregation created a larger-than-life-sized charcoal drawing of Jesus casting a shadow of a contemporary person on the ground. This became a vivid focal point throughout the series as we talked about reflecting Christ.

Visual communication in worship does not need to be traditional painting or drawing; it can be any form of visual expression. One pastor was preaching on Jesus' statement "I am the gate." To illustrate, he placed seven chairs on the platform in a semicircle, invited seven worshipers to sit in the chairs, and then lay down in the gap to explain how a first-century shepherd would literally be the gate of his sheep pen.[4] A friend of mine once asked the worshipers in his church to bring a bag of any kind to worship. During the service, he had them all take out their bags and notice how each one was different. He then proceeded to demonstrate his message, "We Are a Bunch of Mixed Bags," by showing his own bag and pulling out different items one by one that demonstrated some of the paradoxes inherent in our saint-sinner character.

Other visuals can be less specific but just as reinforcing. We have used children's collages, fabric hangings, floral arrangements, and papier-mâché sculptures as effective visual elements. These are just a few examples of the endless ways that congregations of any size can use concrete visual images to connect more effectively with people's minds. As we unleash the gifts of

our unique communities of faith, we will discover new ways to help people
see the truth we are proclaiming.

SYMBOLIC COMMUNICATION

In the recent past, some churches have removed the symbolic imagery of
historical Christianity from their worship spaces in order to create a more
visually neutral environment less threatening to unchurched newcomers.
While this may be more inviting in some instances, in our emerging
culture the generous use of historical symbols often supports our efforts
to reach new people for Christ. As Robert Webber likes to say, "The
road to the future runs through the past."[5] People today are moved not
only by powerful visual images but also by a sense of connection to the
ancient character of our Christian faith. When unchurched people come
to worship, they expect an environment rich in symbolism even if they
do not fully understand the meanings of those particular symbols. Many
growing churches today are rediscovering the rich liturgical heritage of
our faith and are using Christian symbols to connect with the minds of
members and newcomers alike.

Symbolism supports our communication only when it is interpreted at
some level to the worshipers. The cross is the central symbol of our faith,
yet we often miss the opportunity it offers to communicate the means of
our redemption visually. Something as simple as gesturing to the cross while
talking about Jesus' death will make the message more vivid. Look for other
symbols in your worship space. When designing our new worship center,
in addition to a large carved cross, we also included imagery from Revelation
22; the river of life is depicted in a flowing fountain, and the tree of life
is carved into the walls on either side of the fountain and on the chancel
furniture.[6] Whenever possible, we try to refer to these images as visual
reinforcement of our preaching and teaching. How can you use the symbols
in your worship space to help communicate your message more effectively?
If you have a relatively bare worship space, what are some ways you can
begin to introduce biblical symbolism?

In addition to concrete symbols, many churches today are rediscovering
the use of liturgical colors and seasons to enhance the symbolism of their

worship. The visual representation of the cyclical seasons with colors and symbols can provide a sense of rhythm and meaning to worship over the course of a year. The ancient liturgical calendar can be used to provide this seasonal movement. We have adapted the liturgical calendar to support our mission: fall, Christmas, and Easter are outreach-oriented; Advent and Lent are focused on spiritual growth; during Pentecost and Epiphany, we emphasize ministry and service. In whatever ways are helpful to our purpose, we highlight other historical days of the church year (Holy Trinity and Reformation Sunday) as well as cultural "holy days" (Mother's Day, Fourth of July, Thanksgiving). These are not strict, legalistic designations that bind us but a missional structure that provides balance, movement, and rhythm to the content of our worship. We often use the historical colors that accompany the various seasons (red, green, purple, white, black) as well as concrete visual symbols (crown of thorns, flames, angels, butterflies) in original ways to produce a visual sense of this rhythm. These become focal points that create a meaningful environment and provide visual support to our message. The more we are able to interpretively use traditional and creative biblical symbolism, the more we will help people connect intellectually with God in worship.

THEMATIC WORSHIP

One of the most important strategies for reaching people intellectually is to make sure the entire worship service, and not just the sermon, is thematic. A strong theme running throughout the worship experience, tying all the disparate elements together and building conceptual momentum from the beginning to the end, connects people cognitively with the message and has a greater impact on their lives.

Great things can happen when we integrate the biblical theme with the entire service. When the subject of the message is introduced early in the service, begins to unfold via the elements that precede the sermon, is integrated into the proclamation itself, and is applied by the elements that follow, the mind not only receives the truth that is proclaimed but also retains and begins to integrate that truth. This requires complete cooperation and teamwork among the preacher and others involved in leading worship.

This highly thematic approach takes more time, requires a high degree of trust, is often difficult, but results in extremely effective worship experiences. (For more on developing worship orders, see chapter 23.)

Just as building thematic momentum and reinforcement through the course of a worship gathering increases its effectiveness, so building momentum over the course of a multiple-week worship series connects with people's minds. When people come to worship Sunday after Sunday and there are no overarching themes that tie the services together, these services can become a series of disconnected experiences, each leading in a slightly different direction and diluting the impact of the others. When each worship theme builds on the last, taking an important biblical theme far deeper than any single service ever could, people's minds begin to be transformed.

In my experience, in congregations that don't use worship series, most worshipers cannot remember what the theme was from the previous Sunday. When you are using the series approach, you have the chance to reinforce last week's message and lay the groundwork for the next week's. In addition, as you begin each service, you already have the momentum built up from the previous weeks. Worship series also enable you to use creative elements that would be too expensive or time-intensive to use for only one week but can be effective in reinforcing the message of an entire series.

Occasionally, we will do a stand-alone service, but we find the impact of a series is far greater than any group of disconnected worship gatherings. It is not unusual to hear people refer to the way that God used a certain worship series in their lives. Most of our worship series are four to eight weeks long. I find this is enough time to develop significant biblical themes but not so long that people become bored or we end up over-emphasizing one particular subject. There are myriad ways to organize a series. For example, you might choose a specific theme and build on it by using text from a different biblical book each week. Or you can take the opposite approach and center your series on consecutive chapters in a biblical book or from books in a section of the Bible, such as the Prophets. In any case, we try to give every series an imaginative title that will paint a memorable image in people's minds. "Go Against the Flow" was a more effective series title than "The Countercultural Message of the Prophets." (For more on developing series, see chapter 20.)

RESOURCES FOR THE MIND

Another way to engage people's minds more deeply is to sell, at no profit to the church, books that reinforce the message of the service or take that topic further. We have a person on our creative arts team who leads our ministry resources team. When we are brainstorming ideas for a worship series, we also come up with ideas for resources that might help our worshipers go deeper in their understanding and application of the biblical message. After church services, we provide for sale the resources we think are especially effective. For example, if we are emphasizing the importance of studying the Bible, we might have a table of study Bibles for sale immediately after the service so people who don't have a current, usable Bible can get one and start using it right away.

Sometimes we base an entire worship series on a certain book and offer that book for sale so people can go further and deeper with the themes we address in worship. Sometimes we sell other kinds of resources that support the message or the theme, such as music CDs or Bible reference charts. It is usually possible to set up an arrangement through your local Christian bookstore for ordering books on consignment and at a discount. Online booksellers, such as christianbooks.com, might offer deep discounts but usually won't allow you to return unsold books, so orders need to be made carefully. We have sold literally thousands of books this way, at no profit to our church but with great profit for our members. I cannot tell you how many people come up to me months after a series is over and tell me how deeply a book that they purchased at our church right after a service has affected them or changed their lives.

In addition to books, we often give away simple, concrete reminders of the theme for people to take home as a way of keeping in the forefront of their minds that experience and what they learned. This might be a rock, a nail, a lump of clay, a handmade cross, cardstock cut into a symbolic shape with a key Scripture or phrase printed on it, a magnet, or a paper sculpture. Sometimes this is something they actually made during the worship gathering and reflects their personal experience. Months after these particular services, church members have told me they've saved one of the "souvenirs" and told me what it means to them.

LIMITS OF THE MIND

When I was a freshman in college, I took a philosophy class taught by the head of the department who was, at that time in my life, the most learned and intelligent person I had ever come in contact with. In the course of the semester, this professor proceeded to challenge and contradict nearly every Christian belief I had ever held dear. In a matter of a month, I found myself doubting my faith and wondering how I could ever know if the Bible is true. After all, this person knew so much more than I did and seemed to undermine the very basis of my faith! How could I know if the historical claims of Christianity I had come to accept were actually true? How could I know if *anything* was true?

I found my answer in the writings of Paul, who had to face the intellectual challenges of the Athenian philosophers. In his first letter to the church in Corinth, Paul explained the nature of the Christian gospel: "For the message about the cross is foolishness to those who are perishing, but to us who are being saved it is the power of God" (1 Corinthians 1:18). He goes on to explain that human beings were not able to know God through the strength of their own wisdom, so God had to come to us through a "foolish" message, the message of the cross. He tells us that "the mystery of God" has not been revealed according to the demonstrable "signs" that Jews demand or the "wisdom" of the Greeks, but rather through the paradoxical and unexpected death and resurrection of Jesus. Finally, Paul describes the basis of his own faith: "My speech and my proclamation were not with plausible words of wisdom, but with a demonstration of the Spirit and of power, so that your faith might rest not on human wisdom but on the power of God" (1 Corinthians 2:4-5).

I came to understand and accept that my faith could not be based on a certain understanding of God but that it had to be founded on God himself. Once I learned to base my faith on the power of God in my life and adopted St. Anselm's ancient slogan "Faith seeking understanding," I found the freedom to love God with all of my mind through ten more years of higher education and beyond. Our ability to intellectually comprehend God or prove certain truths about him is a shaky foundation for faith because it is always subject to being disproved. The only foundation that cannot be shaken is faith that is based on the power of God to change our lives. The fact that I was a different person because of my relationship with Jesus Christ was the one thing that my philosophy professor could not explain away! The transformation of the followers of Jesus from cowards hiding in an upper room into martyrs ready to die for their testimony of Christ is the greatest confirmation we have of the Resurrection.

In the modern world, Christian apologetics hung its hat on logical reasoning and supposedly objective argumentation. In our emerging post-modern world, this peg has been removed from the hat rack, and we are being challenged to find new ways to convince the world of the life-changing truth of Jesus Christ. This means not that we abandon the mind but that we engage people's intellect along with their senses, emotions, and will so that like Paul, they can say their faith is based on the transforming power of God. Understanding will grow out of experience, and people will come to love God with their minds as they encounter him more fully.

Part Four

Soul Worship:
Engaging and Transforming the Emotions

Jesus began to weep.
John 11:35

Chapter 11

FEELING OUR WORSHIP

A SOUL STORY

As I pedaled the rickety old bike along the road, following an ancient dike, I was still reeling from emotions generated by events of the previous twenty-four hours. I had met Pam a month earlier when I first arrived at the secret headquarters of Eastern European Bible Mission for my stint as a short-term missionary. She had just returned from a trip to Czechoslovakia, smuggling Bibles and Christian books, a full-time veteran of the Mission. While shaking her hand that morning, I sensed there was something different about this woman. How little did I know the implications of that first impression!

In the weeks that followed, we developed a strong friendship, bolstered by long talks, bike rides through the Dutch countryside, and swimming together in the nearby North Sea. Although I tried hard to deny it, there was something much more than friendship growing inside of me. I found myself watching her when she wasn't aware of me, marveling at her beauty and grace. My mind kept warning me, "It will never work—there are too many risks, too many obstacles," but my soul wasn't listening. When the eve of my departure arrived, I took the plunge. On the way home from dinner, I told her how I felt about her and received a polite but noncommittal response. *That's it*, I thought with despair. *After tonight I will never see her again.*

The next morning came early as I departed for my flight home. I was shocked by how deeply grieved I was to leave Pam. It felt like a part of my soul was being torn out. I discovered my flight had been canceled, and wondering if it were fate or chance, I returned to the Mission headquarters that evening. Arriving after dinner, I found that Pam had gone for a swim, as we had become accustomed to doing in the evenings.

Jumping off the rickety bike on the dry side of the dike, I clambered up the steep, grassy slope. As I cleared the top, there she was, coming out of the water toward me. Pam looked like she had seen a ghost and let out a shriek of surprise. That night, we talked far into the morning hours. Eventually, she took the plunge too, revealing her feelings for me, and so began an odyssey of love that has continued through more than twenty years of courtship, marriage, children, and ministry.

NEGLECTING THE SOUL?

I cannot begin to tell you the intensity of emotion that accompanied the roller coaster of proclaiming my love, feeling rebuffed, saying goodbye, being reunited, and discovering a reciprocal love—all in the space of a day! Emotions are a powerful force in human beings and can dramatically shape our lives. The feelings born on that Dutch dike over twenty years ago continue to have reverberating effects in my life every day. As humans, we like to think of ourselves primarily as rational beings, yet emotions often seem to have a bigger impact on our lives than purely calculated choices. We all act in surprisingly irrational ways. How many times have you considered a purchase you knew you couldn't afford but made it anyway? How many times have you said things in the heat of the moment that you never meant and wished you could take back? If reason ruled our lives, there would be no need for psychologists, marriage counselors, and twelve-step groups.

Children are a wonderful reminder of our emotional nature because they have not yet learned to mask their feelings as we adults have. Kids laugh and cry, scream with rage and squeal with delight, all in the space of a few moments. You can watch the emotions play across their little faces like storms on a lake. The teenage years bring another whole range of hormonally driven mood swings. But we are told adulthood is all about learning to control and suppress unacceptable emotions. Instead of dealing with and channeling our feelings, we are trained to repress them. It shouldn't surprise us that many people finally lash out in bursts of destructive anger.

Don't you sometimes watch a child throwing a temper tantrum and wish you were allowed such free expression of emotion? Perhaps we would all be a bit healthier if we programmed a good tantrum into our PDAs every once in a while!

In spite of our emotional repression, we can look back and see what an important part feelings have played in our lives. When I think of my most memorable moments, they are all deeply emotional experiences: getting my horse, my first date, the death of my grandparents, playing for the state football championship, high school graduation, my wedding, the birth of my children, my ordination, my best friend's suicide, the birth of my long-awaited nephew . . . The list goes on and on.

If emotions play a part in the most important events of our lives, why would we ignore this aspect of human experience when planning worship gatherings intended to convey a transforming encounter with God? As good modernists, we were taught not to trust feelings and so to exclude them from our worship planning. We are told faith is to be built on fact, not feeling, so intentionally addressing emotions in worship is considered by many to be irresponsible at best and heretical at worst. The result is bland, lifeless worship that, while perhaps faithful to a certain kind of doctrine, never stirs the soul.

No wonder our young people tell us that worship is boring. People visit and never return. Our members are reluctant to invite their unchurched neighbors and friends. In an age that has seen rationalism founder on the rocks of experiential paradox, we cling to a narrow view of worship that too often relegates the wonder and mystery of our faith to nothing more than a reductionist head trip! While our worship becomes increasingly impotent in the emerging culture, we find comfort in a controlled intellectual exercise or formal ritual practice that is safely devoid of any real passion. Yet when we read the Scriptures, we notice a profound contrast between our bland worship and the passionate, holistic expressions of love for God modeled by biblical people.

EMOTIONS OF BIBLICAL PROPORTIONS

Even a cursory reading of the Psalms reminds us that biblical worship is a profoundly emotional experience.

How long must I bear pain in my soul, and have sorrow in my heart all day long? . . . Turn to me and be gracious to me, for I am lonely and afflicted. . . . Weeping may linger for the night, but joy comes with the morning. . . . You have turned my mourning into dancing; you have taken off my sackcloth and clothed me with joy, so that my soul may praise you and not be silent. . . . Be glad in the LORD and rejoice, O righteous, and shout for joy, all you upright in heart. . . . May those who sow in tears reap with shouts of joy. (Psalms 13:2; 25:16; 30:5,11-12; 32:11; 126:5)

The psalmists repeatedly invite us to express our love to God with strong emotion. There is no "stiff upper lip" here; the feelings of the soul are embraced as a vital part of the language of worship. Notice the great spectrum of emotions represented: sorrow to joy, weeping to rejoicing. There is no screening out "unacceptable" feelings; the soul is laid bare for God to see. Do you ever find yourself shocked by the brutal honesty of certain psalms? When was the last time you used Psalm 137:8-9 ("O daughter Babylon, you devastator! Happy shall they be who pay you back what you have done to us! Happy shall they be who take your little ones and dash them against the rock!") in worship? We sanitize the Scriptures for use in our services, but the Psalms call us to rediscover emotional honesty as a vital part of authentic worship.

It is not just the psalmists who freely express emotion in their encounters with God; we can see this same pattern throughout the Scriptures. An aging and childless Abraham expressed his fear and despair to God (see Genesis 15). The people of Israel "wept before the LORD" for entire days as an act of worship when facing civil war with the tribe of Benjamin (see Judges 20). When Saul was anointed king, the people performed "well-being offerings" and rejoiced before the LORD (see 1 Samuel 11:15). When Hezekiah reestablished temple worship in Jerusalem, the people were having such a good time that they extended the seven-day festival another seven days (see 2 Chronicles 29-30). Have you ever had so much fun in worship that you decided to extend the service another week?

Open expression of emotion is not only a characteristic of Hebrew worship; we also see the same pattern in Jesus and his followers. When Jesus saw the grief of Mary over her brother Lazarus, "he was greatly disturbed in spirit and deeply moved. . . . Jesus began to weep" (John 11:33,35). When Jesus looked out over Jerusalem from the Mount of Olives, he broke down in tears, knowing the destruction that was soon to come (see Luke 19:41). Entering the temple courts, Jesus' righteous anger fueled his radical overturning of the tables (see Mark 11:15). In the Garden of Gethsemane, Jesus was so afraid of the suffering awaiting him that "in his anguish he prayed more earnestly, and his sweat became like great drops of blood" (Luke 22:44).

It wasn't only in sorrow that Jesus expressed intense emotion. Jesus liked to describe repentance as a cause for angelic celebration (see Luke 15:7). At one point, Luke describes Jesus' emotional state when he wrote, "Jesus rejoiced in the Holy Spirit" (Luke 10:21). Jesus said to his disciples, "I have said these things to you so that my joy may be in you, and that your joy may be complete" (John 15:11).

Mary sang for joy at the news of her pregnancy, shepherds and wise men rejoiced when they saw the newborn child, and Anna and Simeon celebrated in the temple at Jesus' dedication (see Luke 1:46-55; 2:20,27-38). The disciples expressed fear in the face of a Galilean storm, became angry at the arrogance of the brothers of Zebedee, and celebrated their success upon returning from their mission trip (see Mark 4:40; 10:41; Luke 10:17). As Jesus was led away to be crucified, the female followers of Jesus wailed openly, and when Jesus died on the cross, the crowds went away "beating their breasts" while the disciples hid in the locked Upper Room "for fear of the Jews" (Luke 23:27; John 20:19). On Easter morning, when the women arrived at the tomb they were "terrified" by an angelic messenger and left the empty tomb "with fear and great joy" (Luke 24:5; Matthew 28:8). Jesus had promised his followers this full range of emotional experiences: "Very truly, I tell you, you will weep and mourn, but the world will rejoice; you will have pain, but your pain will turn into joy" (John 16:20).

Whatever our predisposition toward emotion, it is impossible to deny that feelings comprise a major aspect of who we are as human beings and play a significant role in our faith. The Bible is not simply a dispassionate account of historical facts and theological ideas; it's also a passionate love story, filled with every kind of human experience and emotion. This is not to say that our worship of God should be based on our emotional state at any given moment. Job is the model for the determination to worship God regardless of feelings and circumstance when, after losing everything dear to him, he "fell on the ground and worshiped" (Job 1:20). Obviously, feelings can never be a substitute for the intellectually ascertained basis of our faith or the Spirit-empowered decision to trust the truth revealed to us, but to separate our worship from this critical aspect of human experience is to rob worship of its biblical passion and radically reduce its relevance to our lives. Experiential Worship is the biblical rediscovery of a passionate love song to God that rises from the depths of our souls.

Chapter 12

WHAT ARE WE AFRAID OF?

EMOTIONAL AVERSION

"Quit your whining right now!" "Stop giggling—it's not funny!" "You're just being oversensitive." "Buck up and be tough." "What's the matter with you—why are you so sad?" "You just can't trust your feelings." "Don't be such a baby!" "You'll only get hurt again." "Don't you know that children should be seen and not heard?" "If you don't stop crying, I'll give you something to cry about!"

How were your emotions received when you were a child? How do we respond when babies cry? My first reaction is to try to get them to stop crying: "Shhhhh. Don't cry. It's all right." It shocked me as a young parent when I realized that I was trying to squelch my son's expression of emotion whenever it didn't suit me. Children cry for a reason. It is their God-given way of expressing pain and communicating what they need. Yet how often do we respond with the message that they should not express their emotions in this way? Part of maturity is learning the most constructive ways to express our feelings and putting them in perspective. Yet, overtly and subtly, we often give our children the unmistakable message that all expression of emotion is wrong.

I remember sitting across the dinner table from my sister one night when we were children. We were eating spaghetti. I don't know what got us started, but we were giggling—uncontrollably. Spaghetti-out-the-nose kind of giggling. Our parents had taken about as much of this as they could handle. The threat involved a one-way trip to the bedroom with no meal service and a hint of corporal punishment on the side. An uneasy silence fell over the table. I was employing all my underdeveloped willpower not to look up at my sister. *Focus on chewing and swallowing,* I told myself over and over as I twirled a mouthful of pasta on my fork and shoved it in my mouth. One glimpse of my sister's gleaming eyes and twitching facial muscles was all it took for the bubble to pop. I'm not sure if it hit the far wall, but I vividly remember red sauce on the white tablecloth and a piece of half-chewed pasta stuck to my sister's face.

When was the last time you laughed uncontrollably? If you are like me, it has been far too long. When was the last time you had a good, long cry? Ditto. We've outgrown such silly things. It's just not what mature adults do. We have learned our lessons all too well: *Repress your feelings. Control your reactions. Don't let anyone see what is going on inside. Protect yourself by hiding your heart and soul.* These lessons are taught not only by parents and teachers but also by the painful realities of life itself. The playground, the dance floor, and even the boardroom can be brutal classrooms for the lesson of emotional repression.

I was what you might call "a sensitive child." In elementary school, I spent my recess time in the library rather than on the playground. Part of that was my love of reading, but maybe some of it was my fear of ridicule. I could never find it by looking in the mirror, but apparently somewhere I had a sign permanently attached that read, "Pick on me." When the teasing started, so did the tears. I would try to hide them, but that only made matters worse. "Sissy!" "Coward!" "What's wrong with you?" We are ashamed of our emotions when we've been shamed by them.

I thank God I had a father who was not afraid to show emotion and a mother who accepted my feelings, but even the best family environment cannot protect us from the world. Emotions come on their own timetable, not at our behest. The "wrong" emotions have a bewildering way of popping up at the "wrong" times, don't they? So we clamp down on *all* emotion. We close off a vital part of who God created us to be, and our souls begin to suffocate.

The church is not exempt from this strangulation of the soul. Too often, we have labeled certain emotions as "good" and others as "bad." However, the criteria for this categorization are not so much what is biblical as what is comfortable. Whatever emotions make us feel good are considered acceptable, and those that are troubling are considered unacceptable. We have attached value judgments to feelings and, in so doing, have contributed to the repression of emotion in worship.

Take anger, for instance. Most of us have gotten the idea that anger is intrinsically bad. But in the Hebrew Scriptures, God is sometimes described as angry (see Exodus 4:14). The Gospels portray Jesus, in righteous anger, clearing the merchants from the temple courts (see John 2:15). Paul tells us specifically that we are to learn how to express our anger: "Be angry but do not sin; do not let the sun go down on your anger, and do not make room for the devil" (Ephesians 4:26-27). When Jesus speaks against anger in the Sermon on the Mount, he is addressing the destructive actions that anger can provoke, not anger itself (see Matthew 5:22).

When was the last time you allowed people a constructive opportunity to express God-given anger in worship? Probably never, because we tend to think of anger, along with a slew of other emotions, as being inappropriate in church. Because we cannot control which feelings might be evoked if we allowed our worship gatherings to become emotional experiences, most of us tend to exclude, or at least ignore, the soul as an aspect of worship. That is why our services often feel flat and dispassionate!

Sometimes our resistance to emotional expressions of worship is rooted not in repression but in a reaction to destructive, emotional excess. Some of us bear deep wounds in our soul from emotional manipulation and spiritual abuse. In traditions that emphasize the emotional aspects of our faith, it is sadly common to slip into unhealthy patterns of spiritual elitism, legalism, and counterfeit emotionalism. Genuine feeling can be replaced by inauthentic expressions and manufactured emotion in order to measure up to an unbiblical standard of emotionalism that has based spiritual validity on a certain intensity of feeling. These unhealthy and unbiblical perspectives are diametrically opposed to loving God with all your soul.

EMOTION, NOT EMOTIONALISM

We must make a clear distinction between *emotion* and *manipulation*. Emotion can move people to respond with concrete choices, but it does not overpower their will or mask their ability to decide. Manipulation, on the other hand, coerces people into choices of which they are not fully aware. Holistic, biblical worship will always seek to engage the soul along with the other aspects of human experience but will never use emotion to pressure someone into decisions they are not ready to make. Paul, who understood the power of emotions, was sometimes accused of manipulation, but he was very clear about the integrity of his approach: "We have renounced the shameful things that one hides; we refuse to practice cunning or to falsify God's word; but by the open statement of the truth we commend ourselves to the conscience of everyone in the sight of God" (2 Corinthians 4:2). We will navigate this same road of openness and integrity as we seek to engage the soul in worship.

Some of us are suspicious of addressing the soul in worship, not because we have seen emotional manipulation firsthand but due to accounts of emotionally driven movements that have strayed far from biblical teaching or resulted in great conflict. Maybe you know of churches that have been torn apart or individuals who have been deeply hurt by emotional excess and manipulation in worship. These memories echo in the ears of those who would tell us to check our emotions at the sanctuary door, yet at what price?

From the very beginning of the faith, there has been a risk in opening our souls to God in worship. We need go no further than the Corinthian church to see a vivid example of this. Their worship gatherings changed lives, yet they had become excuses for the rich to exclude the poor, for the spiritual to flaunt their pride, and for all to binge on sacred wine. For good reason, Paul reprimanded them and instructed them to carry out their worship "decently and in order" (1 Corinthians 14:40). This is to be our own standard in worship, yet at the same time Paul affirmed the use of emotionally explosive gifts such as healing, prophecy, and tongues. His point was to use these more emotional aspects of worship for the "upbuilding and encouragement and consolation" of the Christian community (1 Corinthians 14:3). This is the biblical balance of heart, soul, mind, and strength in Experiential Worship.

Some of us may continue to resist the idea that emotions play an important role in biblical worship gatherings. If so, we would be wise to ask ourselves what is holding us back. Worship without emotion allows us to keep God at arm's length and ourselves in control. Biblical encounters with God are powerfully emotional and very risky, yet they produce transformed lives. If we ask God for courage, he will give us strength to turn over control to him and embrace a more biblical attitude toward the soul in worship.

Chapter 13

THE POWER OF EMOTION

TEARS IN WORSHIP

"I want to keep coming, but I just can't anymore." She was a woman who had been attending our church for a month or two. Having only greeted her after worship a few times, I didn't know anything about her, so I was unsure why she had asked to meet with me in my office. "Why can't you keep coming?" I asked. She started to answer but then stiffened. In spite of her best efforts, a lone tear made its way silently down her left cheek. I pushed the well-used tissue box toward her and she buried her face in a tissue as though she were hiding. I waited while she regained her composure. "I don't know what it is, but every Sunday in church I just start to cry."

Somehow encountering a God who loved her unconditionally touched something deep inside that could be expressed only through tears. However, the shame she felt in openly expressing emotion during worship was so great that it was driving her away from the very thing she most longed for. Assuming she was the only person crying in church, she felt everyone was watching her. What she didn't know was that many people cry openly during our worship services, which is why we added tissue boxes to the standard supplies in our pews. I explained to her that emotions are a good gift, a God-given way for us to open our souls in worship, a source of healing, and a means of growth as Christ followers. My words didn't instantly change the shame she felt in crying, but they did give her the courage to continue expressing her feelings to God in worship.

THE IMPACT OF THE SOUL

Tears in and of themselves are not the point, and causing people to cry is not the goal, but something intense happens when our emotions come together with our bodies, our intellects, and our wills in worship. We know that we are sinful, but when we feel remorse, we are moved to genuine repentance. We sing the words of celebration, but when we feel the hope of salvation, we find strength to face our deepest struggles. We hear the call to discipleship, but when we feel inspired, we are led to commit ourselves to a life of service. Emotions can connect our intellect with our will. We have all heard stories of people who, in a moment of mortal crisis, showed superhuman strength by lifting a car off an injured person or performing some other amazing feat. Our emotions can move us to do things we otherwise would never accomplish. When we embrace emotion in worship and begin to intentionally consider how to engage people on this level, we unleash the potential for genuinely changed lives.

During ten years of higher education, I had the opportunity to study under some of the greatest theological minds in the world. I discovered there is no correlation between amount of knowledge and depth of faith. Some of my professors knew far more about God and the Bible than I ever will know yet did not display any perceptible faith relationship with Jesus Christ. For them, it appeared God and the Bible were objects of dispassionate study. Others had just as much knowledge, but their studies had led them to faith because they experienced the truth of that knowledge. They not only *knew* things about God but *felt* things as well, and this led them to respond with various concrete choices and commitments. Spirit-led emotion can make the connection between mind and heart that leads to genuine faith and discipleship.

This is very much what happened to Saul on his way to Damascus (see Acts 9:1-6). As a Pharisee, he knew more facts about God than most of us, yet his life was profoundly out of sync with God's purpose. When he came face-to-face with Jesus, it was an experience so intense that his whole life was changed. He not only came to understand that God had revealed himself in Jesus Christ but also was filled with a passion to follow and serve Jesus no matter what the cost. Paul describes this shift from knowledge to commitment in 1 Corinthians 2:4-5: "My speech and my proclamation were not with plausible words of wisdom, but with a demonstration of the Spirit and of power, so that your faith might rest not on human wisdom but on the power of God." Through our emotions, the Holy Spirit can powerfully connect what we *know* with what we *do* through what we *feel*.

The soul can be a mirror that helps us see deep inside ourselves to places that otherwise would remain hidden. I find that when I ignore my emotions, I sometimes end up acting in ways I regret. When I am more aware of my feelings, I can make deliberate choices to deal with those things rather than being controlled by emotion. The woman I met with in my office didn't know why she was crying during worship, yet those tears were a sign of deep issues that needed to be addressed. Emotions can help us overcome our denial and bring to the surface those things within us that need to be healed, forgiven, released, or transformed. Emotional worship has a prophetic function in helping people to confront their inner brokenness and allow God's Spirit to bring healing and new life.

It is important to remember that emotional worship is born not only in pain but also in joy. The very first two verses in the book of Psalms say, "Happy are those who do not follow the advice of the wicked, or take the path that sinners tread, or sit in the seat of scoffers; but their delight is in the law of the LORD." Happiness, delight, wonder, hopefulness, celebration, gratitude—these are just a few of the emotions that are naturally produced by an authentic encounter with the God of all goodness and grace. It is a mistake to reduce worship to meeting felt needs and making people feel good all the time, but at the same time, the gospel is truly "good news" and as such will have a profoundly positive effect on those who receive it. While it is important to honestly confront the reality of sin and address the struggles of life in a broken world, we are called to also invite people into the joy and blessing of living in the presently emerging kingdom of God.

Sometimes I think we take ourselves too seriously. Our church's teaching pastor, Greg Wallace, has a wonderful sense of humor. Often, as a congregation, we find ourselves laughing uproariously during Greg's sermons and then discover that God has touched us in a deep and lasting way. A Christian community that cannot laugh as well as cry during worship has not yet embraced the full range of worshiping God with the soul. When people leave a genuine encounter with God, they will feel a new hope and a deeper joy, not because the difficult realities of life have been glossed over but because they have been put into a new perspective: the victorious promises of God!

As we learn to create worship experiences that help us express emotions, we will invite the Holy Spirit to connect facts in the mind with commitments in the heart through feelings in the soul. These emotional experiences will bring to light those places within that need the healing touch of the Spirit. In this context, emotional worship is not some kind of entertaining diversion but a mode of real spiritual transformation.

STIRRING THE SOUL IN WORSHIP

I remember preaching my very first sermon as a junior in high school. Stepping up to the pulpit, I felt tremendous excitement about my message—the resurrection of Jesus—yet as I looked out over that sea of faces, I was shocked by how *unexcited* they appeared. It wasn't that they looked sad or hopeful or even confused; it was that they didn't look like they felt *anything*. I figured they would perk up once I got going, but of course I was wrong. It was as if their faces were chiseled in stone. Authentic worship is the most emotion-producing experience there is, yet I discovered early in my ministry how difficult it can be to engage people on the emotional level. Even if we overcome our own aversions to emotion, we have those of others to contend with. Beyond that, we have the obstacle of culture. We often use outdated language and music that no longer speaks to people. Many have become emotionally numbed by the sensory overload of our media-drenched culture. Their souls cannot be reached by our traditional communication methods.

If we counter the false messages of the past and teach a more biblical view of emotion, people will learn to open their souls to God in worship. He has designed us to be emotional beings and wants to use our emotions to guide us, empower us, heal us, motivate us, bless us, and bless others. Through teaching, use of examples, and biblical interpretation, we can help people overcome their fears of opening up. In my church, we often tell stories of people who have experienced God in emotional ways. Sometimes we explicitly explain the God-given design of emotions.

But merely teaching is not enough. A willingness to express our own emotions as leaders is a prerequisite to effectively inviting others to worship God with their souls. If we are unwilling to risk genuine feeling during worship, we will not be able to lead others into soul-stirring experiences of God. This is a challenge for those of us who lead public worship, because we need to maintain a level of control in order to function. But just as with physical worship, people need to see emotional worship modeled by those who lead.

There is no one right way to do this. Each of us has a different emotional makeup. Some of us are more naturally expressive of feelings; others of us have greater control in the midst of our feelings. Each one will learn a different way of expressing emotion during worship in a way that is genuine. Authentic emotions cannot be conjured up or programmed, but we must be open to the process of feeling. I'm not talking about using public worship as a form of personal therapy; I'm talking about being transparent enough that people can see our real emotions and so learn to open their souls to God in worship. Do you let your emotions show while preaching a sermon or singing a song? What if you openly expressed emotion during a part of the service you were not leading? While this might feel risky and there are obviously appropriate limits, this is how we can lead people to a new level of worshiping with the soul.

Chapter 14

ART AND THE SOUL

THE ART OF EMOTIONS

The arts are perhaps the greatest tool available to stir the emotions of our worshipers, because more than anything else, they speak the language of the soul. In God-given artistic expression, reflections of divine beauty become an opening for truth to penetrate the deepest part of a human being and bring transformation. Ken Gire describes how art can become an opening into the deepest part of who we are:

> God gave us art, music, sculpture, drama, and literature. He gave them as footpaths to lead us out of our hiding places and as signposts to lead us along in our search for what was lost. . . . We reach for God in many ways. Through our sculptures and our scriptures. Through our pictures and our prayers. Through our writing and our worship. And through them he reaches for us. . . . When we look long enough at a scene from a movie, a page from a book, a person from across the room, and when we look deeply enough, these moments framed in our minds grow transparent. Everywhere we look, there are pictures that are not really pictures but windows. If only we have eyes to see beyond the paint. If we look closely we can see something beyond the two dimensions within the frame, something beyond the ordinary colors brushed across the canvas of our everyday lives.[1]

Art has the power to reach the emotions as nothing else can. Abraham Heschel said, "A work of art introduces us to emotions which we have never cherished before. Great works produce rather than satisfy needs by giving the world fresh cravings."[2] Words can tap the emotions, especially when used creatively as in a story or poem, but verbal expressions speak more to the mind than to the soul. I may be giving an impassioned sermon on a very sensitive subject, but often it is not until the film clip, drama, dance, or poem that people's emotions are truly engaged and God is able to reach their souls. This use of the arts is not emotional manipulation but an intentional effort to encompass the full range of biblical worship.

Alexandr Solzhenitsyn wrote, "Art can warm even a chilled and sunless soul to an exalted spiritual experience. Through art we occasionally receive—indistinctly, briefly—revelations the likes of which cannot be achieved by rational thought."[3] A new reformation is underway that restores the biblical role of the arts in worship. As we affirm the artistic gifts of our people and empower them in creative teams to help shape our worship, we will discover the life-changing power of inviting people into emotional encounters with God.

When the people of Israel were wandering the Sinai desert, God taught them to worship him using the full range of their artistic expression. Exodus 25–36 describes in minute detail the beautiful ornamentation of the furnishings and tent of the tabernacle. God specifically called two master artisans, Bezalel and Oholiab, to oversee the artistic expression of the community in designing and executing this fantastic worship space—and all this for their "temporary" facilities!

> [God filled them with] divine spirit, with ability, intelligence, and knowledge in every kind of craft, to devise artistic designs, to work in gold, silver, and bronze, in cutting stones for setting, and in carving wood, in every kind of craft . . . with skill to do every kind of work done by an artisan or by a designer or by an embroiderer in blue, purple, and crimson yarns, and in fine linen, or by a weaver—by any sort of artisan or skilled designer. (Exodus 31:3-5; 35:35)

Bezalel and Oholiab were artistically gifted, but their job was to empower the various creative gifts of people from the community who were moved to offer their artistry to God as an act of worship and to enhance the worship of Israel. This is exactly our job as planners and leaders of Experiential Worship. We are called to affirm the creative gifts of our members and create an environment in which their artistic energy can be harnessed to create life-changing encounters with God. Mosaic, an innovative church in Los Angeles, is doing this more intentionally and effectively than any Christian community I know.[4] David Arcos, their director of creative arts, told me that the passion statement of the creative arts ministry at Mosaic is "to design and produce spiritual experiences by empowering artists to become all that God dreams of."[5] What a compelling vision for the arts in worship!

CREATIVE VARIETY

Historically, music has held a place of honor as the preeminent artistic expression of worship because it is a primary language of the soul. For this reason, music will always play a critical role in moving worship experiences. There is nothing that quite compares with singing a meaningful worship song to God. No wonder the book of Psalms found a spot in our scriptural canon! You have probably felt the emotion brought on by a favorite old hymn or a new worship song that has touched you deeply. The words of the song can express something cognitively, to your mind, but the music sings straight to your soul. Martin Luther, reformer and prolific songwriter, expressed the power of music as a worship art when he said, "Except for theology, there is no art that can be put on the same level as music, since except for theology, music alone produces what otherwise only theology can do, namely, a calm and joyful disposition."[6]

However, the artistic expression of our worship need not be limited to music. The Creator of the universe formed us in his own image, so it should come as no surprise that every Christian community has within it an amazing array of artistic gifts just waiting to be unleashed to serve God. When we open the door for these gifts to become the means of leading people into encounters with God, there is no limit to the way that God will touch and transform their souls.

I suggest we retire the term *sacred arts*; I believe it has outlived its usefulness. This terminology falsely implies that there are some types of art or even particular artistic styles that are appropriate for worship while others are not. This is simply not true. What makes a creative expression appropriate for worship is that it finds its source in the God of infinite beauty and reflects that beauty back to us. In her book on art and faith, *Walking on Water*, Madeleine L'Engle writes,

> There is much that the artist must trust. He must trust himself. He must trust his work. He must open himself to revelation. And that is an act of trust. . . . We trust as Lady Julian of Norwich trusted, knowing that despite all the pain and horror of the world, ultimately God's loving purpose will be fulfilled and "all shall be well and all manner of things shall be well." And this all-wellness underlies true art (Christian art) in all disciplines, an all-wellness that does not come to us because we are clever or virtuous, but which is a gift of grace.[7]

God is calling us to go beyond the more familiar musical and verbal arts to rediscover a much broader range of artistic expression in worship. This is what Sally Morgenthaler calls "a tapestry of the arts" in worship. Our job is to weave various strands of creative media into meaningful patterns that engage people emotionally in worship. Morgenthaler describes the whole spectrum of arts as "cultural languages" that move the proclamation of God's Word from the "informational to the affective."[8] While a Bach organ cantata or a sermon by Charles Spurgeon has artistic power to stir the soul, so can a video, dance, or drama. I have participated in worship services that variously included a high school drill team, a stilt walker, and a trash-can band. While these are not the kinds of art we usually think of in worship, each was "sacred" because it was used to bring glory to God and move people into an emotional encounter with Jesus. The arts can help us to both give and receive more fully in worship. As Morgenthaler says, artistic expressions "help reveal God to us" and become "a medium of our response to God."[9]

EMPOWERING ARTISTS

Many of us will be tempted to say, "Well, that's great for a big church like Mosaic located in a highly artistic cosmopolitan setting, but we are just an ordinary church." While this reaction is understandable, it is not biblical. New Testament ecclesiology tells us that every Christian community has been divinely gifted and Spirit-empowered to carry out its unique, God-given purpose (see Ephesians 4:11-13). This means that the church you are a part of—no matter its size, makeup, or location—has all the gifts and resources needed to carry out the particular ministry to which God has called you.

If you don't have anyone who can paint or dance or act or write, it simply means God is not calling you to use that particular artistic expression at this time. Perhaps there are other artistic expressions you never would have thought to use, but once you begin to affirm artistic gifts and empower the unique combination of artists in your community, you will discover those ways of engaging the soul in worship. When you unleash the creative gifts of your community, you will be amazed at the number of artists that come out of the woodwork to fill in the blanks.

THE ART OF WORSHIP

In my church, the nonmusical arts that seem to have the greatest emotional impact are storytelling, drama, and film. All of these are narrative art forms because, as we saw in our discussion of engaging the mind, stories connect us to the "Grand Story" of God. The Bible itself is the story of God and God's purpose for people and all of creation. When we weave stories of all kinds into the worship experience, not only do our minds become more receptive to God's truth but our souls become more receptive to God's touch.

At our church, we tell lots of stories in our sermons, including those from personal experiences; about people we know; and from books, e-mail, and the Internet. Sometimes we have someone read a children's story while its illustrations are shown on the screens; other times we ask members of our congregation to tell their personal stories of faith. Those who plan and lead Experiential Worship will learn to constantly be on the lookout for stories that move people. Our church has one volunteer on our creative arts team who sifts through e-mails for quality stories that relate to upcoming messages.

Drama can be a powerful way to embody stories in worship. A well-executed scene can help people experience the message through every emotion from laughter to tears. Using drama effectively is increasingly difficult in an emerging culture that rejects any form of phoniness. If your themes are established well ahead of time, you can probably find or develop writers to come up with creative dramas that avoid the formulaic feel that many "worship skits" have. Moralistic skits and those that give simple answers don't work. Realistic dramas of five to seven minutes in length with minimal backdrops and props are most compelling. Remember, good drama can be very good, and bad drama can be very bad. *No drama* is always better than poorly done drama. If you do not have the gifts and resources to do drama well, then wait until you do.

Film is perhaps the most effective storytelling tool available to us, and in my church, we use it much more often than we do drama. Movies have become the preeminent art form of our time and affect people in our culture more than any other creative expression does. Mel Gibson's film *The Passion of the Christ* is a perfect example. It masterfully employs the full artistic potential of filmmaking to tell the story of Jesus' suffering with unprecedented emotional impact. Few expressions of explicitly Christian art have had such widespread impact in our time, which underlines the influential role of movies in our culture. A friend of mine expressed it this way after seeing *The Passion of the Christ* for the first time: "Reading the story is one thing, but to see and hear is to be engaged at a completely different level of experience. . . . [It was] powerful beyond measure."

Because tens of millions of dollars are invested in major studio releases, we cannot compete with their production quality, but we can benefit from it. The key is learning to find the right clips to use in the right way.[10] Look for brief scenes that illustrate critical aspects of your message, even for those who have not seen the movie. We like to use three- to five-minute scenes and offer a succinct introduction if necessary. The more people who have seen the movie, the more effective the clip will be, but even obscure films can be potent if the scene has inner coherence. Sometimes we use a clip without introduction to begin worship and then unpack its meaning as the experience unfolds. Other times we use a scene to lead into a sermon, place a scene within the sermon, or intersperse a sermon with multiple clips that build on each other. Often we use serious drama or epics, but comedy can be effective in creating a lighthearted moment, romance can stir up strong feelings, and an occasional action scene builds excitement.

Each congregation will have to wrestle with the issue of using variously rated movies. Using a scene from a movie does not mean you are endorsing the movie itself. Remember, Paul quoted a Greek poet and a pagan altar in his sermon on the Athenian Areopagus without endorsing either the poem or the pagan god (see Acts 17:28). Sometimes after showing a clip from a movie I would definitely not recommend, I'll slip in a comment such as, "You probably won't want to go out and rent this movie, but it does show us that . . ."

Although all my examples have related to forms of story, we are not limited to narrative art. Every form of artistic expression has the potential to stir emotions, and different themes call for different approaches. One Christmas, we focused on the promises given through angels, so our visual arts team created a huge angel Gabriel and hung it from the ceiling of our worship space. One worshiper sent me an e-mail saying, "When I saw the angel Gabriel, it reduced me to tears. I was just so touched by such majesty."

Participating in the creation of art during worship—such as painting, writing poetry, or drawing—can be deeply moving experiences. A friend of mine designed a worship series that utilized the creation of a "Passion Mosaic." With the help of a mosaic artist from their church, participants were involved in breaking tiles, choosing the pieces, mounting them, and grouting the finished mosaic that depicted Jesus on the cross. The entire process was a moving experience that helped the group feel Jesus' suffering for them.

The use of art does not need to be complicated to touch the soul. Sometimes a single photograph that captures our humanity can evoke profound hope or touch long-hidden despair. In our church's worship gatherings, we often use poetry written by gifted members to elicit emotion in nonnarrative ways. Your community of faith is blessed with unique artistic resources that God wants you to discover and unleash in worship. Keep experimenting and see how the Spirit leads your team.

INTENTIONAL CREATIVITY

Just as important as the form of art we employ is the way we use that particular art form in our worship. Like the effective design of a well-constructed sermon in which ideas build on each other and lead to a powerful conclusion, the creative elements of an experiential service should be carefully positioned so that they engage people emotionally and help move them to a place where God can touch their souls. I am talking not about a rigid modernist linearity but about a thoughtful approach of experimenting while avoiding self-indulgent displays of creative excess that bear no fruit.

Emotions are fluid and they build as a result of a process. This means that Experiential Worship services must be designed with connectivity so that we build emotional momentum. Feelings do not usually appear out of thin air. Most often, there are many factors that lead up to an emotional moment. While planning worship services, our team considers what elements will build to a moving moment. *How* we use emotive elements is as important as *what* we use. A comedic drama can open a person emotionally to receiving a significant truth, but if it is used at the wrong time, it can fall flat or even offend someone. A dark and troubling poem can give people permission to open up painful feelings to the healing of the Spirit, but if not properly interpreted, it might leave them confused and only deepen their despair. A moving dramatic film clip can help connect a biblical truth to personal experience, but if it comes too soon in the service, its impact will be lost because people are not ready to experience it.

When the creative elements of a worship gathering are carefully crafted so that they each work in concert with the others, they will help lead a person to an emotional state through which the Holy Spirit can heal, renew, and transform the soul. This is not emotional manipulation but asking the Holy Spirit to guide us in opening a door to the soul. In our worship planning sessions, we often discuss what emotions we think might be generated at a particular point in the worship experience and then consider how this can open people to the transforming work of the Spirit. This helps us decide what elements to include and how to use them to the best of our understanding, but in the end, we trust our mysterious God to work in his own time and way.

THE LIMITS OF EMOTION

In the modern world, emotions were largely discounted. After all, since when did feelings ever show up on an X-ray machine? You can't put feelings in a test tube or measure them with calipers. In an empirically based culture, facts were seen as the basis of faith. This mythical omnipotence of science and logic has been revealed as hopelessly naive in a postmodern world where empirical knowledge and education have not transformed humanity or solved all our problems. The emerging culture recognizes the limitation of scientific reason and is embracing mystery, intuition, and experience as valid, even primary, modes of knowing. Today, people are far more likely to come to faith because of a feeling and then later come to understand the facts behind their faith.

Precisely for this reason, it is important that we recognize the pitfalls of emotionally based faith and carefully compensate for the limitations of feelings by balancing them with the other biblical aspects of holistic worship. As I've already made clear, there is no room for emotional manipulation in biblical worship. Even as we invite people into emotional encounters with God, we are addressing their minds and engaging their wills. This means that Experiential Worship will evoke emotions that empower the will but do not overpower the mind. The goal is never emotions, per se; rather, we are seeking to open people to the powerful way that God can work in us through our emotions.

Emotions will never form an adequate foundation for faith. While emotions are powerful, they are also highly subjective. Biblical worship will never lead people to base their faith on feelings, for feelings change like the weather. They might be as strong as a hurricane and when harnessed can generate tremendous spiritual power, but they can suddenly disappear and leave us emotionally empty. This is when the objective facts of our faith are shown to be the rock upon which our house is built so that no storm can knock it down. No matter how we are feeling at any particular moment, it doesn't change the fact that Jesus is the Son of God, who died on the cross for our sins and rose from the dead to break the power of death and open the way for us into God's eternal kingdom. This kind of unchanging truth forms the bedrock of Experiential Worship.

More and more, people will come to faith and grow spiritually, not just through rational persuasion but as a result of intense physical experiences and deep emotional encounters with the God of mystery and wonder. We are called to facilitate these kinds of experiences even while we teach the objective biblical basis of Christian faith and call people to concrete faith commitments. The timeless truth of the gospel is the foundation of faith that will not waver when our senses deceive and our emotions fade. The beauty of Jesus' Greatest Commandment is that it provides a healthy balance for our worship life. The power of Experiential Worship is that it emotionally engages the soul through the senses of the body while speaking to the mind and appealing to the will.

Part Five

HeartWorship:
Engaging and Transforming the Will

. . . so that you may discern what is the will of God—what is
good and acceptable and perfect.

Romans 12:2

Chapter 15

To Do or Not To Do?

A Story of Decision

The circle of light around my desk seemed to form an arena where my inner angst waged battle with the deepest longings of my soul. Far past midnight, my roommate stirred in his standard-issue dorm bed while I pored again over the pages of my Bible, hoping that somehow a divine revelation would free me from the horns of this dilemma.

From the sixth grade on, I knew my destiny in life: I was to become an equine veterinarian! It fit perfectly with the particulars of my life. I came from a long line of medical professionals. I had always excelled at the "hard" sciences. I loved animals. I had been showing and training quarter horses since I was a kid. I couldn't stand the thought of a "desk job." As a recently declared biology major, I was eating up the challenges of the premed coursework. In my mind, I had already designed the expansive equine health clinic where I would devote my life to veterinary medicine. It all made perfect sense.

By some miracle of psychology, I had managed to fully repress a conversation only one year earlier when I was a senior in high school. My pastor had asked me to meet with him in his office. It was probably the tension built up from wondering why he wanted to talk to me, but I burst out laughing when he told me he believed God was calling me to full-time ministry. Regaining my composure, I patiently explained to him that God was calling me to a life of caring for animals. I shared with him that I would have ample opportunity to minister to the various people with whom this vocation would put me in contact. Confidently leaving his office, I determined not to entertain such thoughts again, never pausing to consider whether *my* plan for the future had anything to do with *God's.*

My freshman year in college had been a season of unparalleled spiritual growth. For some reason, I felt an insatiable hunger for Scripture and prayer and was greedily enjoying both on a daily basis. It was a small-group Bible study, though, that was the primary catalyst for my dilemma. It wasn't the topic we were studying, nor was it something that anyone said. I think it was simply the spiritually charged atmosphere that pried open my heart. There was no booming voice or burning vision—just a persistent sense that God was calling me to something quite different from my imagined clinic. "But I could never be a pastor!" my heart protested. "Who could ever think up something new to say every single Sunday?" The truth was, I felt profoundly unworthy to go into the ministry, and I really didn't want to be a pastor. Besides, there were my cherished ambitions to consider. Giving up on my plans and answering a call to the ministry felt like sacrificing everything. "Would God ask me to give up so much?" I mused doubtfully.

Weeks stretched into months, and the nagging call would not fade away no matter how I tried to ignore it or shout it down. Weary of the battle, I called for a resolution. Committing a month to prayer, fasting, Scripture, study, and counsel, I determined to make a decision one way or another within thirty days. Those days found me praying and reading and seeking the input of people I respected most. My pastor smiled when I told him of my dilemma. "Don't you remember our conversation last year?" he asked. Before he finished the question, that entire memory came flooding back. I couldn't believe it had been possible to repress so completely an event of such significance.

The next morning, I sat down in church and opened the bulletin to discover we had a guest preacher, a tiny seventy-year-old missionary from Taiwan who could barely see over the pulpit. Her text was from the sixth chapter of Isaiah, and as she powerfully repeated the divine inquiry "Whom shall I send, and who will go for us?" (verse 8), it was as if she spoke to only me. Later that day, I met with her for counsel, confiding my feelings of inadequacy, and she shattered my final excuse by showing me various Scriptures confirming that God would provide whatever was needed to answer his call.

As I continued my dorm-room vigil late that night, I moved outside the arena of light and lay down on my bed. My thirty days were almost up, and I had to make a decision. There was no longer any doubt about my calling; the only question was whether I would find courage and faith to answer that call. Peering impotently into the dark veil of my future, I realized that God knew far more than I what would ultimately be best for my life. If he loved me enough to die for me, certainly he would not lead me astray, would not offer a stone when I so desperately needed bread!

I knew it was one of the most important decisions I would ever make, a choice that would radically affect every aspect of my life from that day forward. But I also knew that I would have to choose. No one else, not even God, would do it for me. There was no fanfare or blinding light—only a deep shift in my heart as I made my decision. Letting go of my plans and opening myself to his, with unclean lips like Isaiah, I said, "Here I am; send me!"

At first I was ashamed to tell anyone. Who did I think I was, anyway, imagining that *I* could be a pastor? But before long, I had to explain why I changed my class schedule and declared a new major. As I listened to my voice explaining why I had decided to go into the ministry, deep in my heart I knew that it was the right choice. Gradually, I came to peace with my decision. Today I am grateful every day to be in ministry and can't imagine doing anything else. Sometimes I wonder what my life would be like if I had made a different choice.

THE POWER TO CHOOSE

Every day we make choices—some seemingly mundane, others obviously profound. But every decision, no matter how small, affects the course of our lives. My life would be very different had I chosen to pursue veterinary medicine instead of full-time ministry. If I had decided to stay at the airport when I missed that flight instead of returning to the mission headquarters, I might never have married Pam. If I had decided not to drive back to school late at night, I would not have had a head-on collision with that truck. I knew the decision about my calling had huge implications, but how could I have known the impact of those other "ordinary" choices?

What an amazing and awful thing it was when the Creator endowed his creatures with the power to choose! Why did God impart to us the risky responsibility of decision makers? How much easier it would have been for God and for us if he had simply kept human beings under his perfect control. We would still be enjoying the fruits of Eden in a blissful state of childlike innocence. Or would we? A closer look would reveal the glazed eyes of those children, for without the power to choose, they would not truly be children of God but instead puppets dangling at the end of a faultless string on a tidy stage.

I love my two sons more than words can say. To live in a relationship of love with them and with my wife is my greatest joy in this world. I can guide my sons by my own example, I can make certain decisions for them, I can even force them to obey me, but I cannot make them love me. Only they can choose love. Our Creator knew that the price of authentic love was the risk of genuine choice. In order to make a relationship of real love possible, God had to give us the freedom to accept or reject his love. Adam and Eve were given the power to choose but tragically misused it, and all of creation has been groaning ever since.

Now we live in the paradox of a world ruled by an almighty and purposeful God who has given his subjects the freedom to contravene his perfect will. This dilemma raises age-old questions: *If God is truly omnipotent, how can we have the freedom to make real choices? Doesn't that violate God's absolute sovereignty? We live in a world broken by sin, but if there is no such thing as free will, who is responsible for sin—God? If God is perfectly good, how can he be the source of evil, sin, and death?* This conundrum of free will versus predestination is a debate that has continued unabated throughout the history of our faith.

While I would not presume I could solve this insurmountable problem here, we must address the role of the will in worship because Jesus called us to love God with all that we are, including our wills. To love God with all of our hearts is to make a deliberate choice to give ourselves back to God in response to all he has given us. Biblical worship is the intersection of God's gracious initiative and our freely given response. If God were to coerce our worship, it would be hollow and meaningless. True biblical worship always has its source in the grace of God, but that grace has the power to elicit a response of the will in us.

FINDING BIBLICAL COMMON GROUND

There are very good reasons why we should be wary of overly optimistic views on the freedom of human will. When we naively assume that we are free to make any choice we want, we run the danger of invalidating God's grace and slipping into the legalistic self-righteousness of the Pharisees. After all, if we are free to choose, then sanctification is simply a matter of exercising our willpower—or is it? From his own experience, Paul expresses the limitations of free will: "For we know that the law is spiritual; but I am of the flesh, sold into slavery under sin. I do not understand my own actions. For I do not do what I want, but I do the very thing I hate" (Romans 7:14-15). This is the universal human experience. There are things we can freely choose, but there are significant ways in which our wills are bound in slavery to sin. Anytime the focus in worship is exclusively on our own choices, we can easily forget that our salvation, and ultimately everything good in our lives, is a gift of God's grace. Biblical worship never idolizes human willpower or leads people into the trap of works-righteousness.

On the other hand, our zeal to protect the doctrine of salvation by grace alone can easily become an excuse to ignore human responsibility and avoid engaging the will in worship. A failure to call people to respond to the grace of God is nothing less than the age-old heresy of antinomianism. Paul anticipated this misunderstanding of his emphasis on God's grace when he asked and answered the rhetorical question "What then are we to say? Should we continue in sin in order that grace may abound? By no means! How can we who died to sin go on living in it?" (Romans 6:1-2). Grace that leaves us bound by sin is no grace at all. Worship that ignores the will is worship based on an unbiblical pseudo-grace. As Dietrich Bonhoeffer explained so well in *The Cost of Discipleship*, to offer grace that does not empower the will is to cheapen God's grace and rob the gospel of its life-changing power:

> Cheap grace is the preaching of forgiveness without requiring repentance, baptism without church discipline, Communion without confession, absolution without personal confession. Cheap grace is grace without discipleship, grace without the cross, grace without Jesus Christ, living and incarnate. . . . Costly grace is the gospel which must be sought again and again, the gift which must be asked for, the door at which a man must knock.[1]

Jesus often emphasized the role of the will in authentic worship. It was the widow's decision to give all she had as an offering to God in worship that impressed Jesus so much (see Luke 21:1-4). Jesus made a direct connection between our outward expressions of worship and our concrete decisions that shape the character of our lives. In the Sermon on the Mount, he said, "So when you are offering your gift at the altar, if you remember that your brother or sister has something against you, leave your gift there before the altar and go; first be reconciled to your brother or sister, and then come and offer your gift" (Matthew 5:23-24). Jesus is telling us that deliberate acts of the will are a critical aspect of authentic biblical worship.

Often our discussion of free will ignores the significance of Pentecost, when the power of the Holy Spirit was unleashed in the lives of every believer (see Acts 2:1-13). That day in Jerusalem, the followers of Jesus were empowered to do things they never could have done before—things that ultimately changed the course of human history. Jesus anticipated this when he said, "Very truly, I tell you, the one who believes in me will also do the works that I do and, in fact, will do greater works than these, because I am going to the Father" (John 14:12). When we experience the grace of God, through the power of the Spirit we are empowered to do amazing things, things we never would have dreamed of before.

When Paul wrote to the Philippians, he expressed the paradoxical tension between God's power and our will when he wrote, "Therefore, my beloved, just as you have always obeyed me, not only in my presence, but much more now in my absence, work out your own salvation with fear and trembling; for it is God who is at work in you, enabling you both to will and to work for his good pleasure" (Philippians 2:12-13). Paul boldly called the Philippians to make concrete decisions regarding obedience and salvation. At the same time, Paul made it clear that ultimately this was not their own doing—God was the one who was empowering them to make choices according to his divine purpose. If we hope to lead people into life-changing encounters with God, we will find ways to boldly call for a Spirit-empowered response of the will without denying the sovereignty of God or invalidating his saving grace.

On the eve of my ordination into the ministry, I found myself again wrestling with feelings of unworthiness and insufficiency. At that time, God gave me a promise that has been the basis of my calling ever since: "The one who calls you is faithful, and he will do this" (1 Thessalonians 5:24). God calls us by his grace, we answer as an act of our will, and God provides the power to carry out that call.

WORSHIP AS A RESPONSE

No matter what our views on the paradox of God's sovereignty and human will, we can all agree with the biblical vision that God has called us to exercise our will in worship by his grace and through his Spirit. Every Christian must hear and respond to Jesus' clear call to discipleship: "The time is fulfilled, and the kingdom of God has come near; repent, and believe in the good news" (Mark 1:15). Jesus is calling us to respond to the gospel with faith and commitment.

In the earliest books of the Bible, worship is primarily expressed as the deliberate choice to make a literal offering. We can see this in the very first generation of humanity when Cain and Abel worshiped by offering grain and lambs to God (see Genesis 4:3-4). When Abram and Sarai first arrived in Canaan and received God's promise, they built an altar for offering (see Genesis 12:7). While the people of Israel were still in the wilderness, God instructed them to construct the tabernacle so they would always have a place of offering wherever they went (see Exodus 26).

Even in the New Testament, we see Mary and Joseph making an offering at the dedication of their newborn child (see Luke 2:24), Jesus commending a widow for the proportion of her financial offering (see Luke 21:3), and Paul participating in sacrificial rites at the temple upon his return to Jerusalem (see Acts 21:26). The importance of the concept of offering in biblical worship is measured by its prevalence in Scripture; various forms of the words *offer* and *offering* occur 1,132 times in the Bible. Again and again we see that biblical worship is a deliberate decision to offer ourselves to God.

As Louie Giglio says, "Worship is our response to God. In other words we don't initiate worship, God does."[2] The simple decision to attend a worship service is already an act of the will, an offering of our time and availability to God. When we lead worship, we lead people who already have made a choice to worship. Will we invite, challenge, and empower them to continue to take steps toward a deeper and more complete experience of worship? Failing to lead people beyond their initial decision to attend a worship service is to miss a life-changing opportunity.

In his pivotal book *Celebration of Discipline*, Richard Foster lays a critical foundation for the role of our will in all transforming spiritual exercises. He begins by clarifying that we cannot change ourselves by our own willpower; only God can do this by his grace and through the Spirit. The point of spiritual disciplines, however, is that we can make certain choices that put us in the place where God's Spirit can do this life-changing work. Foster writes, "The Disciplines allow us to place ourselves before God so that he can transform us."[3] He explains that our decision to worship is a spiritual discipline that allows God to transform us in this way. He sums it up by saying, "Worship is our response to the overtures of love from the heart of the Father."[4] As we choose to respond to these overtures from God, we enter more fully into genuine worship.

Chapter 16

INVITING A RESPONSE

WHAT SHOULD WE DO?

If it is to be biblical, each worship experience that we plan will invite people to a very specific response of the will. As we seek to stir deep emotions in the soul, offering a multisensory physical experience for the body and solid biblical content for the mind, the Spirit will empower worshipers to respond to God's grace with the heart in concrete ways. Luke described the people's response after the very first Christian worship experience on the Day of Pentecost: "Now when they heard this, they were cut to the heart and said to Peter and to the other apostles, 'Brothers, what should we do?'" (Acts 2:37). People's hearts were deeply affected, and they expressed a desire to respond. Do the worship gatherings we plan lead people to respond in some concrete way? As we consider various topics for worship, the elements by which we seek to convey them, and the order we design for them, a critical question to ask ourselves is "Will this cut people to the heart and evoke a response of the will?"

When the people asked, "What should we do?" Peter said to them, "Repent, and be baptized every one of you in the name of Jesus Christ so that your sins may be forgiven; and you will receive the gift of the Holy Spirit" (Acts 2:38). Peter called people to specific, concrete actions in response to a powerful experience of God in worship. His call included symbolic as well as functional acts that would help people experience more deeply the message of God's transforming grace and would offer the power to put their faith into action.

Even if our people do not literally ask, "What should we do?" it is a question that resonates in the heart of every person who has an authentic encounter with God. When God touches our hearts, we *want* to respond out of love and gratitude. Too often, our worship services leave people unclear about where to go from there. The historical function of the sending at the end of the service is to send people out into the world with a clear understanding of what they are to do in response to what they have experienced. How often do people go home on Sunday saying things such as, "That was an interesting sermon" or "The choir sure sounded good today" with no thought of what they are going to do differently because of their experience in worship?

PLANNING FOR RESPONSE

When planning a service, can you articulate what you are hoping God will do in the lives of your people? As we design the order and flow of a service, it is important to consider which elements will help move people from receiving to responding. Usually, the responsive elements will come after the primary message or near the end of the service.

I have found that it often works well to place a responsive element immediately after the conclusion of the sermon. If it is a convicting message, we might invite people to kneel and confess their sins to God and then to stand to receive the assurance of God's forgiveness. If it is a salvation-oriented message, we might follow with an opportunity for people to respond by professing faith out loud through the words of Scripture, an ancient creed, or a thematic profession of faith written specifically for that service. If it is an encouraging message, we might follow with a set of very uplifting songs and explicitly invite people to joyfully celebrate God's goodness. If the message is a call to serve others, we may follow with a video describing a mission project or service opportunity. Sometimes it is effective to end the entire service with an invitation to act immediately by signing up for some specific program or event related to the theme. In any case we always close our services with a blessing and sending that reinforces the response we are encouraging people to make.

No matter the design of the worship experience, it is essential that the preacher call for a response to the proclamation of God's Word. Even the best diet of biblical preaching will not birth new Christians or develop strong disciples if there is no practical application of biblical truth. Failing to specifically and explicitly invite people to put the message into action in their lives will simply produce spiritually fat people, not Jesus followers ready to face the challenges of this world. In every sermon I preach, I always try to include some concrete ideas for how to apply the message. This does not mean we reduce preaching to some kind of simplistic how-to seminar. Biblical preaching is always an invitation to encounter the mystery and wonder of God through his Word, centered on the good news of Jesus Christ. Worshipers today are hungry for a deep, authentic biblical message. But if we only offer ideas and never help people respond to the message, they will leave just the same as they arrived.

It is important to be suggestive, not proscriptive, when it comes to practical application. Every person is unique and at a different point on the journey of faith. People in our culture are seeking a message custom-made for their lives. I try to be specific enough that they understand ways the message can be applied but general enough that they can apply it in ways that fit their unique situations. It is also important not to communicate the wrong message when suggesting specific applications. People can easily slip into thinking, *If I just do this one thing, then I finally will have arrived spiritually.* Experiential Worship invites a concrete response but constantly guards against legalism, externalism, and the persistent tendency to judge others. It is easy to fall into the trap of equating spirituality with certain external applications rather than remembering that the gospel will work itself out differently in the life of every person.

Each worship experience should have some element that invites the worshipers to take a responsive step during the service itself. Sometimes this step will be an *internal* response, such as making a personal commitment to God or participating in a time of responsive prayer. At our church, we incorporate confession and forgiveness into our worship on a weekly basis. If used intentionally, this can be a great internal responsive element, but there are other ways to invite this kind of response. Providing a time of silence in which people are invited to reflect on the message and talk to God can be very effective.

Other times you will want to invite people to make an external response of some kind during the worship gathering. In our ministry, we celebrate Communion on a regular basis and, if taught and introduced intentionally, it can be a deeply meaningful form of outward response. Because we normally invite people to come forward to receive the Lord's Supper, we consider this a form of altar call. Sometimes we use a response card to facilitate an outward response. Asking people to write out a response to God on a special card or to check a box indicating a decision can be an effective kind of outward response. Inviting them to bring a response card forward and lay it at the foot of the cross can intensify the impact of this kind of a response. Some churches have asked people to seal a written commitment to God in a self-addressed envelope to be mailed back to them unopened at a later date as a form of self-directed accountability. Many congregations do something like this for their annual pledge drive; why not use it for other kinds of commitment as well?

Inviting people to participate in symbolic acts can elicit genuine and heartfelt response. Symbols speak to deep truths that lie beyond words, and when we invite people to take symbolic actions, they are able to participate in the symbol itself. For their Thanksgiving Eve service, one church had as a visual focus a large, rustic cross with bare branches "growing" from its upright beam. The service compared the barrenness of our lives without Christ to the blessings of fruitfulness that God has poured into our lives. During the sermon, the worshipers were invited to write a prayer of thanks on a paper leaf they had been given upon entering. After the message, they were invited to come forward during a time of singing praise to God and hang their leaves of thanks on the bare branches of the tree. Right before their eyes, the seasonal process of fall was thrown in reverse, and the barren tree was transformed by an offering of thanks.

On Good Friday, a church focused its service on the price Jesus paid to destroy the condemning power of sin. Worshipers were invited to write down their specific troubling sins on 3x5 cards as an act of confession. At the end of the service, people silently filed out of the building onto the patio and threw their lists of sins into a fire that was burning at the foot of a cross. What a powerful act to claim the promise that Jesus' death destroys the power of sin! The church that used an unfinished puzzle of the globe to represent our unfinished call to serve those in need handed out a puzzle piece to each worshiper. The worshipers were then invited to come forward and offer their puzzle pieces to God if they were ready to commit themselves to participating in God's plan for the world.

These kinds of symbolic responsive elements are what I described in chapter 6 as "whole-body experiences." Here we see the body and the will coming together. When someone comes forward to light a candle, place a stone, drive a nail, or lay something symbolically before the cross, it is a concrete way to respond to the Word of God. There are countless ways we can invite people to respond with outward, symbolic acts during worship that will become avenues by which the Holy Spirit can make lasting changes in their lives. These are things that can be done by nearly any size of church without lots of expensive equipment or technical staffing. All it takes is a commitment to engaging the heart, a willingness to unleash people's creativity, and an openness to the leading of the Spirit.

BEYOND WORSHIP

While response is a part of every Experiential Worship service, it is helpful to look beyond the worship gathering itself to find ways of reinforcing a response to the message. Events and programs in the life of a congregation often can offer opportunities for people to put what they are experiencing in worship into practice in a broader context. By coordinating worship series with the launch of new programs or publicity of various ministries, we can capture the momentum of an otherwise isolated worship experience and translate it into sustained spiritual growth. The phenomenally effective program "40 Days of Purpose," from Saddleback Community Church, is based on this premise.[1] Through this program, tens of thousands of churches have discovered that by focusing all the programs of an entire congregation on intensively seeking God's purposes for forty days, the impact of the worship experiences based on those purposes is dramatically magnified.

There are many simple ways to connect a response in worship to the wider ministry of your church. For instance, if you are planning a series on serving others in the name of Christ, why not coordinate it with the registration for your upcoming Mexico mission trip? That way you can offer people a specific way they can put the call to serve others into action. If you are about to launch a new small-group ministry, try leading up to it with a series on building Christian community through small groups. During the series, you can publicize the new groups that are forming and invite people to sign up for them. If you are encouraging people to be more intentional about studying Scripture, you could advertise a new series that is starting at the midweek Bible study. In our church, we try in every way possible to connect our worship themes with our programs and vice versa in order to create natural and effective opportunities to engage the heart in a response to the message. The more we are looking at the big picture and coordinating our overall ministry emphases, the more people will be able to sustain their responses with ongoing spiritual growth.

Special events can also provide effective response opportunities. If you are scheduling a special event in your congregation, do you consider what is happening in worship and look for ways to connect the two? For instance, during a series on marriage and family, we organized a renewal of wedding vows, complete with a fancy reception and photographer. One-fourth of our worshipers participated and had an exciting opportunity to respond to a message on renewing their marriage covenants. It was a meaningful evening that none of us will forget, partly because it grew out of an experience of God in worship.

Holidays also can serve this kind of a responsive function. Because Christmas and Easter are the most visitor-intensive days of the year, why not focus your special outreach efforts around those days and seasons? In our church, we include the beginning of the school year in this category, so every September, Christmas, and Easter, we arrange special outreach emphases. During the weeks leading up to these seasons we highlight the opportunity to invite unchurched friends. On the actual holiday, we plan a service that is especially aimed at the needs of the unchurched newcomer, often giving away a special gift that reinforces the message and invites them back. That service is the first in a series that is designed to encourage those newcomers to return and to introduce them to a relationship with God. Our hope is that if they have a positive, moving experience on Christmas or

Easter or the Sunday after Labor Day, they will be open to coming back for the rest of the series in the weeks following.

One Christmas we centered the service on the idea of going home to God through the birth of Jesus. For our central metaphor, we used a dramatic reading of Max Lucado's parable about a girl named Madeline, from his book *He Chose the Nails.*[2] It tells the story of a young woman named Madeline, whose shame over her lifestyle causes her to become estranged from her father. He sends her many letters, which remain unopened. It isn't until he seeks her out that she finally accepts his personal invitation to come home on Christmas Eve. This contemporary prodigal parable became a way to help people accept the Christ of Christmas, who came in the flesh to invite them home. In addition to inviting newcomers to return the following Sundays for the rest of our "Coming Home" series, we gave each person Max Lucado's booklet *He Did This Just for You,*[3] which contained the story about Madeline and explained the gospel in a clear, engaging style. Each book was gift-wrapped in Christmas paper, and inside was a card outlining the topics of the rest of the series and inviting the person to come back. One Easter a church focused on the historical evidence of Jesus' resurrection. After the service, they handed out copies of Lee Strobel's book *The Case for Christ*, which addresses critical questions about the true identity of Jesus. Inside the book was an outline of a worship series in which they would be tackling these questions and an invitation for them to return.

Handouts can be used to stimulate concrete responses in all kinds of worship gatherings, not just holiday services. For instance, during a series on prayer in which we are hoping people will respond by incorporating a quiet time into the regular routine of their lives, we might print a simple devotional journal, hand it out on the first Sunday of the series, ask people to use it during the week, and then have them bring it back each Sunday to use in the service. Sometimes when we are encouraging people to live in a constant state of prayer, we will hand out small colored dot stickers and invite people to stick them on the center of their watch faces. Each time they look at their watches, they are reminded to be in constant prayer. Occasionally, we hand out refrigerator magnets to remind people of the theme of a series. For one series on God's promises, a church handed out a different magnetic ray of the rainbow each week with the Scripture reference of the promise for that week. The magnet was used to hold a card with all of the promises printed on it to help people memorize the promises one week at a time. From time to time, for each week in a series we print a memory verse on a small card and invite people to carry it with them that week to help plant that Scripture deep in their hearts.

In addition to creating things for people to take home, you can also offer various resources for them to buy that will help them translate their experiences of God into action. In chapter 10, I described our ministry resources team and the strategy of providing books and other resources to help people progress beyond the actual message and go deeper in their faith. This helps people keep responding to the message long after the worship gathering is over.

Chapter 17

What Kind of Response?

By Grace and the Spirit

The Pharisees emphatically called people to exercise their wills by making moral choices. The Sadducees emphasized ritual observance while ignoring moral responsibility. Jesus rejected both approaches and invited people to transcend both legalism and antinomianism. He boldly called people to repentance and a righteousness that "exceeds that of the scribes and Pharisees" (Matthew 5:20).

Jesus' call to repentance was an invitation to participate in the coming kingdom by responding to the grace of God. He invited a clear act of the will as a response to a lavish display of grace. Jesus not only proclaimed the transforming power of the good news but also demonstrated the coming kingdom as he touched the untouchable, healed the broken, released the possessed, and fed the hungry. Again and again, people joyfully responded to this tangible grace by believing in Jesus and following him.

If we hope to see lives changed through experiences of God in worship, we will learn this same art of proclaiming the gospel in such a way that God's grace draws people to respond. Guilt trips, pressure tactics, and manipulation to coerce people's wills are not the ways of Jesus. Such means rob the gospel of its power and disqualify ourselves as ministers in Jesus' name. Likewise, if we fail to help people truly love God with all their hearts by responding in worship, we forfeit our calling as well. One way of balancing this grace-based call to respond is by making sure the opportunities we offer for a response are always optional. When people know they are free to respond or not respond without judgment, their responses will be more authentic and they will sense the gracious nature of the invitation.

The gospel is an intrinsically transforming power and thus always calls for a response. However, the resulting spiritual transformation is a process that happens over time. We do not control this process, nor does it operate according to our timetable. Often it is our own impatience, need for control, and pride in tangible results that lead us to coercive tactics. As we learn to trust God's timing and the work of the Holy Spirit, we will take the responsibility of graciously challenging people to respond in worship but leave the results in God's capable hands.

STORIES OF GRACIOUS EMPOWERMENT

A certain prominent citizen of Jericho had been hearing the rumors for days: "The rabbi from Nazareth is coming!" When the crowds began lining the main road, he guessed the rumors were true: *They say he speaks with authority about a kingdom where even sinners can be made right with God.*

Zacchaeus tried to push his way through the crush of bodies to see what was happening, but he had been at a physical disadvantage all his life. Maybe that is why it seemed worth it to suffer the condemnation and rejection of everyone he knew in order to attain the power of a tax collector for the Romans. When the men who had bullied him as a child now had to pay *him* the heavy fees levied by Caesar, it seemed to almost make up for the humiliation he had suffered at their hands. Backed up by the point of a Roman sword, he had learned how to collect far more than was required and so enjoyed the luxury afforded by his overzealous efficiency.

Now no one would even talk to him, much less let him through to see Jesus, but Zacchaeus suddenly had an inspiration. Just as he had climbed the Roman bureaucracy to get a head up on his enemies, now he grabbed the branches of a tree and swung himself up. From his leafy vantage point, he could see Jesus and the disciples making their way along the road through the sea of onlookers, closer and closer to where Zacchaeus sat. It surprised everyone when Jesus stopped and looked straight up at the little tax collector. Brilliant eyes of divine wisdom looked into his heart, and for the first time,

Zacchaeus knew that nothing justified the sordid betrayal of his fellow Jews. Bracing himself for a well-deserved rebuke, Zacchaeus couldn't believe his ears when Jesus simply said, "Hurry and come down; for I must stay at your house today."

My house! he thought. *Why would the greatest rabbi in the land want to share table fellowship with the most notorious sinner in Jericho?* He could already see indignation on the faces of the pious religious leaders who had expected Jesus to honor them with his presence. But there was no time to marvel at this incomprehensible mystery. Zacchaeus's heart beat wildly as he swung down from the tree and led Jesus to his home. He would throw a banquet befitting his messianic guest!

Things went remarkably well. Jesus wasn't priggish and uptight like most of the religious people Zacchaeus had met. He seemed to genuinely enjoy the party. And there was something about Jesus that shed light on those dark places Zacchaeus had tried to keep hidden. Leaning with an elbow on his pillow at the low table, Zacchaeus listened to Jesus speak, and the words seemed to penetrate his very heart and soul. He hadn't planned to do this, but suddenly Zacchaeus stood up at the table and made an announcement to Jesus and all who could hear him: "Look, half of my possessions, Lord, I will give to the poor; and if I have defrauded anyone of anything, I will pay back four times as much."

There was an audible gasp in the room. Zacchaeus wasn't surprised; his reputation for being a selfish and greedy man was well earned. Even now there was a part of his businessman's mind that was calculating how much this was going to cost him. But it didn't seem to matter anymore. Any amount seemed like nothing compared to the priceless gift Jesus had given him by accepting him as he was and calling him to something better. Then Jesus said to Zacchaeus, "Today salvation has come to this house because he too is a son of Abraham. For the Son of Man came to seek out and save the lost." The words rang like a bell in his newly lifted heart: a son of Abraham. A strange determination welled up in Zacchaeus's heart to live up to Jesus' words, and he knew his life would never be the same. (adapted from Luke 19:1-9)

From tax collector to philanthropist! What if our worship gatherings had this kind of impact on the people who attend? Coast Hills Community Church experienced this when they gave out a hundred-dollar bill to each of one hundred volunteers, with the mandate to use it for a "kingdom assignment." The results were so phenomenal they wrote a book chronicling the effects.[1] A couple of years ago, we did a worship series we called "Pay It Forward," and we tried the same thing, inviting twelve people to come forward voluntarily during our services, each to receive a hundred-dollar bill. They were instructed to "pay it forward" by using that money to do something significant for someone, asking that person in turn to pass on the blessing to others.

It was amazing to see the impact of this responsive worship element on the members of our congregation. The people who received the money were excited to be able to use it to help others. Many of them added their own money and solicited money from others to increase the impact of their projects. One person provided care packages for abused women in a local shelter. Another established a book and video library for children in a local cancer ward. Someone else used the money to put together a craft fair, with all of the proceeds going to a worthy cause.

The even more amazing part was that others who didn't come forward that day initiated their own "pay it forward" projects, creatively making a concrete difference for others in the name of Christ. A few months later, we showed a video with clips of the people describing how they had used their hundred-dollar bills and what they had experienced. This set off another wave of creative initiatives in which people responded of their own volition with acts of service.

A year later, a donor contacted me and asked if we could do it again, so we announced "Pay It Forward 2." Although we did not emphasize it as much as the year before, it also set off a chain reaction of grace-filled acts of love in the name of Jesus. This time, one woman solicited donated material, recruited the help of others, and with her hundred dollars was able to produce over a hundred handmade teddy bears, which were personally delivered to residents of a local VA hospital, sharing the love of Christ face-to-face. Space limitations prevent me from describing all the other amazing, creative ways that people responded to the call to "pay it forward," but the ripple effects are still reverberating for Christ's kingdom.

Every authentic encounter with Jesus will cut to the heart and elicit a powerful response of the will. If we are engaged with God in body, soul, and mind, our hearts will respond with concrete choices. We may fall down as Peter did and say, "Go away from me, Lord, for I am a sinful man" (Luke 5:8). We may run to our friends and neighbors as the Samaritan woman did and say, "Come and see a man who told me everything I have ever done!" (John 4:29). Or we may stand up as Zacchaeus did and joyfully announce, "Half of my possessions, Lord, I will give to the poor" (Luke 19:8). If people in our worship gatherings are not asking, "What should we do?" as they did at that first Christian worship service in Jerusalem, then we have not learned how to engage their hearts in worship. But if people experience an encounter with God in which their physical senses are engaged so they understand profound biblical truths and are stirred by deep emotions, they will be empowered to make concrete *choices*, which will result in changed lives.

Part Six

MAKING IT HAPPEN! A PATHWAY FOR IMPLEMENTING EXPERIENTIAL WORSHIP

Little children, let us love, not in word or speech, but in truth and action.
1 JOHN 3:18

Chapter 18

OVERCOMING ROADBLOCKS
TO CHANGE

THE CHALLENGE OF CHANGE

The thoughts and feelings swirled inside of me like a tropical storm: *Why are they so angry? I thought this is why they called me here! We worked so hard to reach consensus. People were excited about these changes! The votes were unanimous. Why are all these people leaving the church? What did I do wrong?*

If you have ever tried to implement major changes in worship, then you know the thoughts and feelings I am describing. It seems nearly every pastor or worship director I have talked to has "been there, done that." In our case, we tried hard to prevent conflict and division, but in the end, it didn't seem to matter. Sure, we made mistakes along the way and there are plenty of things we could have done better, but the bottom line is that changing the worship culture of any congregation is messy.

Changes in worship are the most risky and painful kinds of change in the church because worship is the most sacred aspect of our life together. This should not surprise us; worship is why we were created and what we are destined for. I am excited and passionate about helping people develop Experiential Worship, but I will be doing everyone a disservice if I skip over the inevitable conflicts that arise from implementing this kind of worship. There is no magical formula for preventing the conflicts or eliminating opposition to change, but we can identify three key roadblocks on the way to Experiential Worship: our radically changing cultural context, failure to understand the purpose of biblical worship, and the confusion about form and content in worship. By considering some specific strategies, we can find ways to overcome these roadblocks and implement Experiential Worship by the grace of God.

THE ROADBLOCK OF CULTURAL REVOLUTION

Culture is the world of symbols that we construct in our own time and place to make our lives understandable. Worship is always expressed in a particular cultural context. Early Israelite worship was expressed in biblical Hebrew, involved the ancient Near East ritual of animal sacrifice, and was adorned with the artistic expressions of first the tabernacle and then the temple. The first Jewish Christians worshiped in Aramaic, gathered on the Sabbath, and utilized the format of the synagogue. Early Gentile Christians worshiped in Koine Greek, gathered on Sundays, and formed house churches. Each group worshiped in a way that reflected its own unique culture. The First Council of Jerusalem, as recorded in Acts 15, made a critical decision. The apostolic leaders of the church determined that Gentile Christians did not have to adopt all the cultural practices of Jews in order to worship God and follow Jesus. Each generation of Christians ever since has had to redefine the relationship between their worship and their particular culture.

If worship does not relate to a particular culture, it will become meaningless. This does not mean that culture should define the content of our worship—in fact the opposite is true. As we learn to utilize contemporary culture to express the timeless message of the gospel, we will become the shapers and redeemers of culture.[1] H. Richard Niebuhr's classic *Christ and Culture* points to this with insightful categories: "Christ *against* culture," "Christ *outside* of culture," "Christ *as* culture," and "Christ *transforming* culture."[2] When we pit our faith against our culture, we condemn the people we are called to reach. When we live our faith outside of the culture, we ignore the people we are called to reach. When we offer a faith that is the same as our culture, we capitulate to the people we are called to reach. When we proclaim the Jesus who alone can transform a culture and those affected by it, we find the balance of a faith that is both countercultural and culturally relevant.

The primary challenge of relating worship to culture is that we are aiming at a moving target. What was popular yesterday will be out of style tomorrow. What meant one thing last week means something different this week. The challenge is to express the timeless content of biblical worship in forms that are meaningful in this changing context.

This challenge is greatly magnified in our own time because for us cultural *evolution* has become cultural *revolution*. We are in the midst of an era of radical cultural transition. Pastor Brian McLaren sums it up: "You and I happen to have been born at an 'edge,' at a time of high 'tectonic activity' in history—the end of one age and the beginning of another. It is a time of shaking. Yesterday's maps are already outdated, and today's soon will be too. The uncharted world ahead is what we will call 'the new world on the other side.'"[3] Professor Eddie Gibbs describes this cultural shaking as a storm that churches must learn to navigate. He writes, "These storm fronts do not simply represent a short-term threat churches must survive in order to return to the familiar and more tranquil conditions that they have previously known. Rather these storm fronts represent a boundary line that separates two very different worlds."[4] The sooner we cross that boundary and awaken to this new world "on the other side," the sooner we will be able to make the changes necessary to invite people into life-changing encounters with God.

There will always be those who are not able to make these kinds of cultural transitions and those who care more about their familiar forms of worship than conveying the content of Christ to new generations. Conflict is inevitable. But if we are diligent in doing what we can to open people's eyes to the cultural revolution happening all around us and faithfully teaching them the missional imperative of cultural relevance, those who are committed to the Great Commission (see Matthew 28:18-20) will begin to embrace worship shaped by the Greatest Commandment.

Read the books I have quoted and anything else you can find on this cultural transition. Preach the principles of Paul's commitment to "become all things to all people, that I might by all means save some" (1 Corinthians 9:22). Demonstrate a willingness to make missional changes in your own cultural comfort zones. Proceed prayerfully. Explain the biblical reasons behind the changes you are making. Build consensus in your leadership, but don't wait for unanimity in your membership. Be ready to face entrenched opposition and be willing to lead through conflict to a place of unified purpose. Build a support network with people you can trust. Above all, seek God's will in everything and maintain a vital relationship with Christ. The cost of changing with the emerging culture is great, but the benefits are even greater. Developing Experiential Worship that engages the whole person helps set the stage for your congregation to act as an agent of changed lives for many postmodern generations to come.

THE ROADBLOCK OF UNCLEAR PURPOSES

Once we address the roadblock of our changing cultural context, the next obstacle we face is confusion over the biblical purpose of public worship. In part 1, we saw that true worship is a bidirectional encounter with God: God comes to us with his grace and love, and we respond to him with our love and commitment. God is the focus of our worship, but we are the ones changed by the encounter. Worship is first of all directed toward God, but today many people have sought to understand the purpose of biblical worship in the lives of those who worship.

Many churches assume that worship is exclusively intended for the edification of Christians and so tailor the details of their services to the needs and preferences of their members. This can be called the "Christian Country Club" paradigm. Every aspect of worship is determined by answers to the question "What do our members want?" The result is an exclusive format that feels foreign to the newcomer and is unintelligible to unchurched people. In reaction to this insiders' approach to worship, the seeker-service movement of the eighties and nineties challenged the church to reconsider the purpose of our worship. In this model, the congregation's primary public gathering is directed no longer toward God but toward the unchurched people who attend. This can be called the "Evangelistic Event" paradigm. Every aspect of worship is determined by answers to the question "What do unchurched people want?" The result is a presentational format that focuses on communicating the gospel to unbelievers but ignores discipleship and actual worship of God. Both paradigms miss the biblical purpose of worship by emphasizing one aspect to the exclusion of another.

The Bible makes it crystal clear that public worship is intended for both the believer and the unbeliever (see 2 Samuel 22:50; Psalm 96:3; Isaiah 66:19). Sometimes in our zeal to reach seekers, we have, like Esau, exchanged the birthright of true worship for the "stew" of presentations masquerading as worship (see Genesis 25:33-34).

Sally Morgenthaler prophetically recognized this mistake and called us back to our biblical roots in her defining book *Worship Evangelism*. She reminds us that throughout the Scriptures, worship is described as encompassing both believers and unbelievers. Morgenthaler calls this biblical inclusion of unbelievers "open worship" and points out that in the Mosaic Law, God gave specific instructions regarding the role of "aliens" in the worship life of Israel.[5] She goes on to point out that Paul instructed the Corinthian church how to conduct worship in light of the needs of unbelievers who were present:

> If, therefore, the whole church comes together and all speak in tongues, and outsiders or unbelievers enter, will they not say that you are out of your mind? But if all prophesy, an unbeliever or outsider who enters is reproved by all and called to account by all. After the secrets of the unbeliever's heart are disclosed, that person will bow down before God and worship him, declaring, "God is really among you." (1 Corinthians 14:23-25)

The extraordinary thing about this passage is that Paul not only affirms the presence of unbelievers in worship but also instructs the Corinthians to consider the needs of these seekers in designing the service and explains that they will be drawn to faith by sensing the presence of God among those who are genuinely worshiping.

God is always the object of biblical worship. Both believers and unbelievers will be changed when they are invited into authentic experiences of God-centered worship. Until our members understand that biblical worship must be designed with the needs of both believers and unbelievers in mind, many will not accept the changes necessary to accomplish this. Our job is to teach a more biblical paradigm for worship that balances these purposes in a deeply spiritual but openly inviting physical, emotional, intellectual, and volitional encounter with God.

As we begin to design and implement Experiential Worship for both believers and unbelievers, there will be no way of pleasing everyone if we are determined to please God. Overcoming the roadblock of confused purposes requires determination. Teach a balanced biblical worship paradigm. Demonstrate a genuine passion to reach the lost and a deep desire to disciple the found. Accept that some will leave, but trust that many more will come. Rediscover your own passion for authentic, God-centered worship, and express a contagious love for Jesus that flows from your heart, soul, mind, and body. As you balance the purposes of worship in holistic encounters with God, you will know the joy of unbelievers coming to saving faith and believers growing as disciples of Christ, and all who witness it will say, "God is really among you!"

The Roadblock of Confusing Form and Content

Our heritage, personality, learning styles, tastes, and experiences all contribute to the style of worship we prefer. When these are combined in deeply meaningful encounters with God, we become attached to the particular style or format of those experiences. Often we come to express these deep attachments in terms of value judgments such as "I believe worship should be . . ." or "True worship is always . . ." Rather than describing biblical principles or spiritually substantive aspects of worship, we often point to the arbitrary styles or formats in which we had these formative encounters with God. Instead of holding on to the transforming content of these worship experiences, we often cherish the form in which they came to us. The result is a subtle kind of idolatry in which we focus on outward expressions of worship rather than on God, who is the substance of all transforming worship.

When Jesus was talking to the Samaritan woman, she hoped to distract him from her living situation by bringing up the primary worship conflict of that time: "Our ancestors worshiped on this mountain, but you say that the place where people must worship is in Jerusalem" (John 4:20). Refusing to take the bait, Jesus instead pointed her beyond the outward forms of worship to its true content: "The hour is coming, and is now here, when the true worshipers will worship the Father in spirit and truth, for the Father seeks such as these to worship him. God is spirit, and those who worship him must worship in spirit and truth" (John 4:23-24).

God does not care whether we worship him in Jerusalem or in Samaria. He does not care if we use pipe organs or rock bands. He couldn't care less if we gather in a cathedral or a coffeehouse. It matters not to God whether we wear robes or suits, cross ourselves or raise our hands. What matters to God is whether or not we are ushering believers and unbelievers into worship gatherings that enable them to experience the truth of Jesus Christ in the power of the Spirit and so be changed. It is time for us to put the old traditional-versus-contemporary debate behind us for good! God can change lives through a highly liturgical service employing organ music and historical hymns as easily as through a high-tech multimedia service filled with the latest worship songs, as long as those outward forms are connecting people—heart, soul, mind, and body—to the transforming content of worship: God.

I love chocolate. As kids, my sister and I always woke up on Easter morning to baskets filled with green grass and all kinds of sweets. I would immediately begin sifting through the jelly beans, hard candy, and marshmallow puffs to find the real deal: chocolate. Sometimes I would find chocolate molded into the form of a bunny. Other times I would find chocolate molded into the form of a chick. Frankly, I didn't care what the shape was; all I cared about was the chocolate! Someone who turns up their nose at a chocolate chick and says, "I only like bunnies!" obviously is not a lover of chocolate. They care more about the outward form than the actual content. The same is true of many worshipers and worship leaders today.

The forms include the language we use, the style of our music, the order of the service, and the various elements we include in that order. While important, these forms of worship are means to a greater end. The purpose of these forms is to convey the content of worship: an authentic encounter with God. The content is the experience of conviction, grace, forgiveness, love, commitment, and joy that comes to us through the forms we employ.

Ultimately, the content of worship is God himself. If our forms of worship are not leading believers and unbelievers more fully into an awareness of God's presence, they are no longer fulfilling their purpose and must be changed.

Most of the conflicts that arise over worship are rooted in a failure to make a clear distinction between the outward forms of worship and its transcendent content. Not realizing this, people understandably feel we are destroying something sacred when we make changes to the expressions of their worship. God is calling us to become chocolate lovers again, who love chocolate so much we are willing to mold it into whatever shape will help people taste its goodness. Our job is to teach the difference between the form of worship and its content so that our members can understand and accept the necessary changes that need to be made in order to make our worship more experiential.

If you are considering implementing Experiential Worship in your church, be sure to address these roadblocks with the staff and leaders before you begin leading people through these kinds of changes. Unless you have strong unity among the leadership, you will not be able to deal with the inevitable conflicts in a healthy and effective way. If you are not the primary leader of your church, be sure the person in that position has embraced the vision and purpose of Experiential Worship before trying to implement it. A worship director or associate pastor cannot make these kinds of changes without the buy-in of the senior pastor and governing board. Ask the decision makers to read this book, and then sit down together to talk about how Experiential Worship fits into the purpose of your ministry. As you develop unity of purpose among your leadership, move ahead with prayerful anticipation.

Chapter 19

FROM THEORY TO PRACTICE

BILL'S STORY

Bill rolled over and looked at the clock. 6:15 already? Why is it that Monday morning comes so much earlier than the others? Dragging himself out of bed, he stumbled into the bathroom and splashed cold water on his face. Blinking away the sleep and meeting his own bleary gaze in the mirror, Bill immediately began to wonder what on earth he was going to preach on *this* week. Every Monday seemed the same: after finishing the Sunday services, he would collapse into bed and then wake up only to face another week with the inevitable services waiting at the other end. More than anything, Bill wanted the worship at this church to be meaningful and powerful, but week after week, it all seemed to fade into a blur.

Hurriedly dressing, he knew how it would be when he got to the office: quickly glancing over the songs chosen by the music director for that week, opening his Bible hoping for inspiration, and praying. It felt like the proverbial treadmill that is moving so fast you can't get off; the only way to stay on your feet is to keep running as fast as you can. The Sundays just kept coming with relentless regularity, like the beat of telephone poles passing the car window. It wasn't that Bill couldn't come up with things to talk about each week. But looking at the faces of his congregation, he had the sinking feeling that what he was saying didn't matter much to them.

After worship was over, he would think of things he wished he had included. He especially hated it when the music director or one of the choir members would come up to him and mention a song that would have gone "perfectly" with the sermon. Bill's daughter had recently gone with some friends to the local megachurch, and her glowing report only made him feel worse. He knew they were in a rut—he didn't need to be reminded. He tried to be creative and come up with new approaches, but sitting alone in his office, all he could think of were ideas that seemed an awful lot like "same old, same old." Recently, he had talked to the music director about meeting regularly to share ideas and plan worship together, but they were both so busy that it seemed they would never make it happen. He knew there had to be a better way, but finding it was another story.

BREAKING THE CYCLE

Bill's story is all too common. So many of us are barely hanging on from Sunday to Sunday. We know that planning and leading worship is the most important thing we do in a week, but so many other things end up crowding it to the bottom of our list. We want people to have a fresh, vital encounter with God every time they gather for worship, but six days is just not enough to prepare these kinds of experiences week after week. Maybe you've been thinking as you read this book, *This all sounds good in theory, but we could never do it at our church.* Or maybe you feel you could marshal your resources and come up with an experiential service once in a while, but to do this kind of worship on a regular basis seems close to impossible.

Planning and implementing Experiential Worship is no simple task, but it is within the reach of every pastor and leader who is willing to develop a process of planning and implementation. The key to developing Experiential Worship on a weekly basis is getting off Bill's treadmill. As long as we start on Monday to plan for Sunday, we will never get ahead of the relentless crush. Sitting in an office by ourselves and trying to plan worship gatherings will never get us out of our well-worn ruts. The key is to break out of the cycle of our solitary, Sunday-to-Sunday routine and develop an ongoing and effective worship-planning process.

Henry Ford understood the importance of a process. By involving many people in a carefully designed process, Ford could produce high-quality cars at an affordable price. None of us wants to settle for the low-quality solo method of worship planning. In a postmodern, post-Christian world, we can no longer afford this approach. Involving more people in a long-range process will enable us to create fresh new experiences of worship, inspired by the Holy Spirit, on a weekly basis. This means expanding our base of resources for creative worship and then organizing those resources more efficiently.

Some might balk at the idea of an organized process for developing worship, thinking this replaces the work of the Holy Spirit. The preferred approach of such critics is for a person to sit alone in an office and pray for the Holy Spirit to guide him or her, with the result being the service that God wants for that Sunday. At best, this is a profoundly unbiblical approach. Assuming that one person, such as a pastor or music minister, has some kind of special conduit to the Holy Spirit by virtue of his or her title or position is to miss the whole point of Pentecost. Both the prophet Joel and the experience of the first Christians in Jerusalem make it clear that the Holy Spirit is at work in the lives of all who believe: "Even on the male and female slaves, in those days, I will pour out my spirit" (Joel 2:29). A biblically based approach that involves many people in the process of prayerfully seeking the guidance of the Holy Spirit is likely to produce a more complete understanding of God's will for worship than any one person can.

The most efficient process in the world is worthless if it does not produce the desired results. The worship we hope to develop will be rooted in Scripture, centered on Christ, and empowered by the Holy Spirit. It will be relevant to local and emerging culture, while addressing the needs of believers and unbelievers alike. Above all, it will intentionally engage people physically, emotionally, intellectually, and volitionally in a direct encounter with God. Inviting people into these kinds of life-changing experiences on a weekly basis will require a pathway made up of steps that:

- Begin with Scripture to assure solid biblical content
- Involve many people in a creative brainstorming process
- Organize implementation of usable ideas
- Design an order for worship that effectively conveys an experience
- Equip leaders to facilitate life-changing encounters with God

- Promote a learning culture that improves and maintains our effectiveness

I can relate to Bill's treadmill because I have "been there, done that." I'm grateful to say that with the help of God, in our church we have broken out of that cycle, and I don't *ever* want to go back. Being a part of an Experiential Worship ministry has been the greatest blessing of my professional life. My passion in writing this book is to help people like Bill break out of the Monday-to-Sunday cycle and discover the joy of inviting believers and unbelievers into life-changing experiences that empower them to love God with all they are.

In this final section, I will describe the process our church has developed. We are not some megachurch with a staff of hundreds, and I am not one of those "super-pastors" who leaps tall buildings in a single bound. We are ordinary people in an average-sized church who are seeking, by the grace of God, to answer an extraordinary call together. I offer concrete examples to stimulate your thinking, not to suggest that you should do it the way we do, but in the hope that it will help you envision what can work in your setting.

Chapter 20

STEP ONE: WORSHIP THEMES

WHERE DO WE BEGIN?

Throughout my years of college and graduate school, I built houses during the summers. I worked primarily as a framer, which meant my job was to come on-site once the foundation was cured and begin building the structure of the house, the floor, the walls, the roof, and so on. I became vividly aware of how crucial the foundation was to the rest of the house. If the foundation was out of level, it was very hard to build a level house. If the foundation was out of square, the house would inevitably end up skewed. A house is only as good as its foundation.

The same is true of our worship. Jesus taught us to build our house upon the rock (see Matthew 7:24-25). The prophet Isaiah reminds us, "The grass withers, the flower fades; but the word of our God will stand forever" (40:8). In our efforts to be culturally relevant, it can be tempting to begin our process of planning worship with some "cool" idea or the latest cultural fad. To do so is to build our house on shifting sand, and sooner or later it will come down. Likewise, in a time that is characterized by bewildering change, it can be reassuring to fall back on familiar formulas or structures for worship based on our denominational history or personal background. This too is shaky ground that can easily crumble under the weight of our current cultural challenges. In the ever-changing realm of culturally relevant Experiential Worship, there is one foundation for worship that will last: the Word of God.

IDENTIFYING THEMES

Our worship planning process begins by prayerfully identifying biblical themes that we believe are currently important for our congregation or wider community. The teaching pastor and I meet periodically to pray, discuss what we see as current issues or needs in our setting, and brainstorm ideas about biblical themes or passages to emphasize. Occasionally, to get more input or feedback on ideas, we will broaden this discussion to include our worship planning team, made up of two or three other staff members. If you do not have more than one pastor or other ministry staff members to include in this process, you might consider forming a team of your most biblically literate and spiritually mature members to periodically discuss current congregational needs and possible biblical themes for worship. In order to allow enough lead time to properly develop these themes, we try to look from two to six months ahead.

As I mentioned in chapter 16, we have developed an annual cycle of worship emphases based on the three aspects of our mission: invite, grow, and serve. These thematic cycles help us maintain a balanced biblical diet in our worship over the course of a year and connect our preaching directly with our mission. We usually choose biblical themes aimed at newcomers (invite) in the fall, at Christmas, and at Easter. We focus on spiritual growth and discipleship (grow) for the seasons of Advent and Lent and after Easter.

ANNUAL CYCLE OF MISSION-BASED WORSHIP THEMES

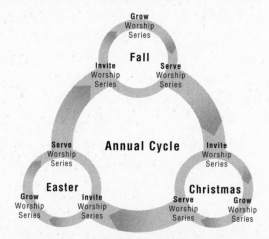

During November and Pentecost, we generally emphasize our biblical call to ministry and mission (serve). Throughout the summer, we try to do something totally different, such as addressing current issues, following a biblical theme, or even responding to questions raised by our members.

Some churches are accustomed to using the ecumenical lectionary, a three-year cycle of assigned Scripture readings, to provide this kind of biblical balance. If you have been doing this for a while, you might want to try developing your own mission-based lectionary, as we have done, or at least use the lectionary as a starting point, giving yourself the freedom to cast a wider net to encompass your current contextual needs. If you have not used any method in the past to provide for healthy balance and variety in the biblical content of your worship, you might want to try developing some kind of a cycle or at least a list of topics you believe are important to cover in the course of a year. When we don't look carefully at the big picture of our worship themes, inevitably we all return to our favorite passages and topics, leaving our congregation deprived of a balanced biblical diet.

Once our worship planning team has developed a biblically based worship series, we distribute a "Worship Themes" packet to everyone involved in the creative aspects of worship (see appendix A for an example). This document lists the series title and an overview of the series. Then for each week of the series, it lists the topic for that week, biblical text, sermon title, synopsis of the message, other ideas for biblical content, any music ideas, and any initial creative ideas. We try to distribute the "Worship Themes" packet about six weeks before the start of a given series in order to allow the necessary time needed for developing creative experiential elements. This is an effective way to get the information about an upcoming series out to a broader base of staff and volunteers so they can begin to prayerfully consider how they might use their gifts to help create an experience of God based on these biblical themes.

It takes a lot of time and effort to create the "Worship Themes" document six weeks before a series begins, but it pays huge dividends and is the critical foundation on which the entire house of Experiential Worship is built. Don't give in to the temptation to say, "I can't afford the time to do this." The truth is, you can't afford not to!

Chapter 21

STEP TWO: CREATIVE COLLABORATION

THE END OF THE IVORY TOWER

Many of us are used to climbing the ivory tower and there, alone in the presence of God, planning the worship of our community. As we have seen, climbing down from our ivory tower, locking the door, and throwing away the key are the first steps toward implementing Experiential Worship. This means recovering the biblical model of collaborative creativity. Jesus carried out his ministry by forming a relational small group focused on ministering together. We are called to do the same. The four men who brought their friend to Jesus through the roof (see Mark 2:1-12) offer an excellent model for this kind of ministry. They united around a common purpose and by working together were able to make a life-changing difference for their paralyzed friend. None of them could have helped this man alone. Even if they could have dragged him to Capernaum on a cart, I'll bet none of them alone would have thought to take him down through the roof (or would have had the courage to do so!).

There is something about being together that stimulates creativity. While creative ideas can come to us in isolation, we are limited to our own set of experiences, insights, ideas, and perspectives. When we come together in an environment of openness and acceptance, our creative palette is dramatically enlarged and we imagine things otherwise beyond our reach.

CREATIVE BRAINSTORMING

Years ago we formed a creative arts team, and we have had a wonderful journey ever since. This team consists of leaders from various other teams, such as music, drama, dance, visual arts, ambient arts, digital arts, film, video production, and literature. Also on the team are people with unique creative passion or experience in production and the staff members responsible for worship, including the preaching pastors. All the members of this team receive the "Worship Themes" packet and are given time to read it over before our meetings and prayerfully think of creative ideas to help people experience God through the truths we are trying to convey.

About one month before a particular worship series begins, we gather for a long evening of creative brainstorming. We break into small groups and brainstorm creative ideas for each week in the coming series. We follow the three universal rules of brainstorming:

1. The sky's the limit—share every idea no matter how outrageous
2. No evaluation allowed—save your critical comments for later
3. Stay focused—limit yourself to ideas related to the topic

We reinforce rule number one with what we call the "Elephant Principle." This means that no idea, no matter how outrageous (such as having an elephant walk down the center aisle), is out of bounds, because such "impossible" ideas give rise to other, more reasonable ideas. By explicitly affirming that even outrageous ideas spawn more usable ones, we are encouraged to go outside the box. When someone is venturing a truly radical idea, he or she often will preface it by saying, "Now this is just an elephant idea, so don't laugh!" Another approach is to put your hands over your head with fingertips touching and request an "umbrella of mercy." This is a reminder of rule number one and a special request for acceptance of an improbable idea.

To enforce rule number two, some people like to use soft foam "killer balls" strategically placed in the center of the table. If someone slips and inadvertently responds to an idea with a critical comment, everyone promptly picks up the balls and hurls them at the offender in defense of the one wronged. This serves as an effective reminder for those who would otherwise dampen the creative spirit.

Rule number three highlights the importance of an effective facilitator who can lead these brainstorming sessions and gently guide us back to our purpose when the creative energy has sent us bounding down a rabbit trail. When one or two people dominate the conversation, this leader draws out the less extroverted and serves as timekeeper so that we can cover the material we need to in the time we have.

At this meeting, we do not discuss which ideas can or will be used; there will be time for that later. Instead, we just enjoy the process of collaborative creativity. It is amazing to watch what happens at these meetings. We come up with powerful metaphors, discover thematic connections, and develop unique approaches to themes that none of us ever would have thought up on our own.

Creative collaboration requires trust, cooperation, and a large investment of time and energy. Some say they cannot afford the time for these creative meetings; I say you can't afford *not* to take time to unleash the creativity of your community. Others say they do not have artists in their church; I say there are artists hiding in every congregation who don't yet know their gifts can be used to enhance worship. Still others resist this kind of process because they are afraid to share control of the worship planning process. As a recovering control-aholic, I tell you that I understand. But the Lone Ranger approach to ministry is a dead-end street, and the only way to develop Experiential Worship is by inviting others into the creative process. It takes a variety of people to create worship experiences that speak to a variety of people. The more people we invite into the creative process, the more people we will be able to reach.

Chapter 22

STEP THREE: IMPLEMENTATION

FROM IDEA TO REALITY

So far, all we have talked about are ideas, but ideas are ultimately worthless if they are never transformed into tangible reality. Unleashing the power of the arts and the creativity of collaboration leaves us with far more ideas than we could ever use in worship. This means that we need a method for sifting through the voluminous results of our brainstorming sessions and deciding which elements will be included in a given service.

Our church does this through our worship planning team, which is comprised of the senior pastor, the teaching pastor, the programming director, and the music director. In our case, these happen to be paid positions, but they could just as easily be volunteers. This is a group of decision makers. They are equipped to decide which ideas will be most effective for our purposes and whether we have the resources to implement them.

We meet soon after the creative brainstorming process so that the ideas are still fresh in our minds. We ask the following questions when considering each idea:

- Will it engage people physically, emotionally, intellectually, or volitionally with the message?
- Will it give people an opportunity to respond to God physically, emotionally, intellectually, or volitionally?
- Is it aimed primarily at believers or unbelievers?

- Does it relate to current culture?
- Is it compatible with our congregation's value system?
- Do we have the resources to implement it with quality?

The answers to these questions help us decide which ideas to implement in a given service. We want to make sure there is an appropriate balance in the elements we choose. If a service is highly intellectual, we try to include some effective emotive elements. If we have lots of elements that engage the physical senses, we want to make sure there is an opportunity for people to respond with an act of their will. If the series or service is focused on outreach, we will emphasize the needs of newcomers, whereas if it is a discipleship series, we will lean toward the needs of our members. No matter what the theme, we always try to ensure the service will be a meaningful experience for believers and unbelievers alike.

We look for elements that are highly relevant to people in our culture today. If the creative elements don't speak the language of the culture at some level, they won't be effective. However, "culturally relevant" does not necessarily just mean "contemporary." Some of the most effective elements can utilize ancient forms of spirituality as long as they are used creatively and presented in a way that unchurched people can participate in them with meaning. We often use traditional elements—such as the stations of the cross, centering prayer, or foot washing—but try to present them using fresh, creative approaches with enough instruction so people can understand them and experience them in meaningful ways.[1]

We also try to balance the cultural relevance of each element with the values of our congregation. We want elements that will be meaningful to unchurched people, but we don't want to offend our members, either. It is important to make the distinction between elements that are inappropriate according to our values and the objections some people have because they are not used to certain experiences in worship. For example, some people object to video projection in worship simply because they "don't like it." We can help these people accept such an element by explaining the missional imperative of using the primary art form of our time to communicate to people in the emerging culture. On the other hand, if we show a film clip that is overly violent or sexually explicit, we have crossed the line from relevance to moral compromise. This balancing act requires courage and lots of prayer to navigate successfully.

The last criterion is often the first considered: Do we have the resources to implement it with quality? Many of our ideas fit all the other criteria and would be very effective in conveying an experience of God but are simply out of our reach. It is important to consider this realistically so that you don't deplete your budget or burn out volunteers. It is better to do less and do it well than to overextend your ministry teams or budget. Start slowly and build your resources for Experiential Worship over time. As people experience God more completely in worship and see the creative arts used to glorify God, they will be motivated to use their gifts to make this kind of worship a reality. As your leadership comes to understand the importance of reaching new people and discipling your members through holistic worship, they will begin to budget for the resources necessary.

IMPLEMENTING CREATIVITY

Once we have decided which ideas we will implement for each week of a series, we send out a revised version of the "Worship Themes" packet, which we call "Creative Themes" (see appendix B). This document lists the creative ideas we will try to implement for each service, identifies a team or person responsible for seeing that item to completion, and gives deadlines. Sometimes there will be multiple teams working together on more involved elements. We utilize e-mail as much as possible to facilitate good communication.

In our case, the programming director oversees the process of implementation. This is a position we created to direct three main aspects of our Experiential Worship ministry: the logistical, technical, and creative aspects. Although I have been focusing on the creative aspect of this process, the resulting ideas require both logistical and technical support in order to be implemented effectively. It is extremely helpful to have someone with strong organizational skills coordinating these three aspects and overseeing all the complex details of various volunteers as your Experiential Worship ministry develops. We didn't start with a programming director and neither will most churches, but it is an excellent position to establish as a volunteer role until a paid position can be afforded. The programming director follows up with various team leaders to see how things are progressing and help deal with problems as they arise.

Teamwork is the single most important key to the implementation process. We have benefited greatly from using the "fractal team model" described by Wayne Cordeiro in his book *Doing Church as a Team*.[2] Fractal teams are small enough to be efficient, focused enough to be effective, and flexible enough to grow and change with your ministry. A fractal team is formed by identifying a missional purpose and a person to lead the effort to accomplish that purpose. The selected person identifies the four key functions that are needed in this effort and recruits four people with the specific gifts needed for those functions. These five people form a team. Once any one of the four areas grows large enough to require more than the time and resources of that one person, instead of adding people to their team, that person forms a new fractal team and becomes its leader. This person clarifies the purpose of the new team and identifies the four functions necessary to accomplish that purpose. After recruiting four people on the basis of their gifts, this person leads the new fractal team and continues as a member of the original team. The beauty of this structure is that each team remains a manageable size, while the teams as a whole can grow to effectively carry out a ministry no matter how large or complex it becomes.

(See appendix D for an example of how this structure can be implemented.)

Like any ministry model, you will want to modify and adapt the fractal team structure to work for your circumstances. We have applied the fractal principles flexibly and the result has been better communication, higher volunteer morale, more effective implementation, and higher quality worship elements. In our structure, the senior pastor leads the worship planning team, made up of the teaching pastor, the music director, and the programming director. The music director leads the various teams responsible for the musical aspects of worship: the choirs, the worship singers, and the worship bands. The programming director leads the welcome team, the technical arts team, and the creative arts team. The various creative teams are led by members of the creative arts team and are the ones who implement the creative ideas for worship. The teaching pastor leads the teams focused on our spiritual growth ministries but is on the worship planning team because he participates in the preaching.

You will define the roles and structure according to the unique scope, focus, and needs of your ministry. If you have fewer paid staff members, you will want to break down the responsibilities into smaller pieces so they can be handled by volunteers. Be clear about the roles, and structure them in such a way that creative ideas can efficiently be translated into reality on an ongoing basis. As you empower gift-based teams, you will begin to see those ideas impacting lives in worship week in and week out.

FRACTAL TEAM STRUCTURE

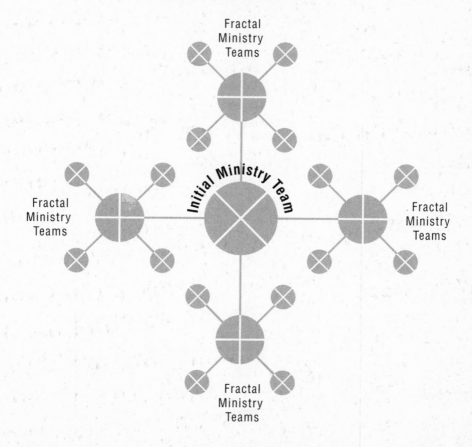

Chapter 23

STEP FOUR: DESIGNING AN ORDER

A WORSHIP ROAD MAP

Pam and I used to work in Eastern European missions, before the fall of Communism. We would travel to countries such as Czechoslovakia or Romania to secretly deliver Bibles and Christian books to church leaders who had no access to such resources. Often we would be covertly trying to find a home in a town or village at night, only to discover that our map was wrong. Because they are often out of date or simply of poor quality, Eastern European maps will not necessarily get you where you need to go, no matter how carefully you follow them. The same is true of the way we structure our worship services. We might have a transforming biblical theme, moving music, reinforcing thematic elements, and colorful expressions of creative arts, but if these components are not put together in the right way, we will not be very effective in helping people open themselves to the life-changing power of the Holy Spirit.

A map is not a place. A map is simply an attempt to show people how to get to the place it depicts. A worship order functions in exactly the same way. We cannot change people's lives, but we can design worship experiences that will lead them down the road to a transforming encounter with God by engaging their hearts, souls, minds, and bodies.

ORDERING OUR WORSHIP

Orthodox and Catholic churches have developed an elaborate structure for their worship based on biblical themes, ancient traditions, and theological convictions. There is a deep sense of connection to the God of history through the rituals and symbolism of the liturgy. Charismatic and Pentecostal churches have a spontaneous, free-flowing approach to worship, conveying a strong sense of God's presence and power in the here and now. Many so-called "nonliturgical" evangelical churches have a very consistent liturgy: opening song set, announcements, pastoral prayer, sermon, and closing prayer. As different as traditions are from one another, they all have a certain kind of structure and order that governs their worship.

Some traditions claim that a certain historical structure is the correct way to worship, while others insist that having any set structure at all compromises the spiritual sincerity of true worship. I do not believe there is a "right" way to order Christian worship. A more elaborate liturgy can convey rich imagery and ensure good, biblical content on a weekly basis but also can be confusing and feel distant. A simpler structure can be easier for new people to follow and allows for more flexibility but also can result in one-dimensional worship that becomes boring or shallow over time. A consistent structure develops a familiarity among worshipers that allows them to move beyond the outward forms of the service and lose themselves in more meaningful expressions of worship. The downfall of consistency is that the forms of worship can become rote and people sometimes slip into "going through the motions." A more spontaneous worship order creates a sense of anticipation and sincerity in worship but also can result in inconsistent worship that prevents the worshipers from deeply appreciating what is happening because it is always unfamiliar.

THE CONTENT OF EXPERIENTIAL WORSHIP

When looking back at the history of Christian worship, there are certain essential elements of worship that have been used consistently throughout the ages and across the spectrum of our faith:

Invocation/Benediction/Charge: Clarifying near the beginning of the service whom we are worshiping, and proclaiming God's powerful blessing and calling to the congregation at the end of the service.

Confession/Absolution: Being honest with God and each other about our failings and shortcomings and hearing the authoritative promise of our forgiveness through Christ proclaimed out loud.

Hymns/Songs/Chants/Anthems: Musical expressions of praise and thanksgiving that recognize both what God has done and who he is; the songs can be *about* God or *to* God and can be sung *to* the congregation or *by* the congregation.

Litanies: Spoken corporate expressions similar to hymns/songs that allow the congregation to speak with one voice.

Prayers: Spoken and unspoken expressions of prayer addressed directly to God by individuals or the congregation as a whole. This includes prayers of adoration and intercession.

Scripture Readings: Readings from God's Word addressed to the congregation.

Preaching: Proclaiming God's Word to the people.

Profession of Faith: A corporate expression of Christian faith meant to define and remind us who we are.

Offering: Giving our tithes and offerings as a response to God's grace; a tangible expression of our decision to offer our whole selves over to God's guidance and purpose.

Holy Communion: The promise of forgiveness and salvation through the celebration of the Lord's Supper, comprised of bread, wine (grape juice), and the words of institution.

Holy Baptism: The promise of forgiveness and salvation for a new member of the community through the application of water and God's Word.

Creative Expression: Employing our God-given creativity through the arts to express praise to our Creator. The most common form of this is music, but worship embraces all of the arts, including drama, dance, visual arts, poetry, film, and video.

These elements represent the core content of worship. They are not listed in a particular order, nor is there one right way to utilize them. It isn't necessary to incorporate every one of these elements into every worship service. This list is more of a menu, and each item simply represents a different "food group" from the history of Christian worship. Each tradition and congregation will be led to develop unique expressions of worship. If we are willing to learn from history and implement these essential elements in creative, culturally relevant ways, we will provide a balanced spiritual diet of worship for our people.

EXPERIENTIAL WORSHIP ORDERS

Although my own congregation comes from a more liturgical tradition, we do not follow a consistent order in our Experiential Worship. We use what we call the "blank page" approach to develop a thematic structure for each service. No two services are ordered in exactly the same way. We want the biblical focus of the service to determine the structure of the service rather than presuppositions about how a service is "supposed to be" ordered.

As we plan the order of a service, we ask, "How can we arrange the unique combination of elements for this week into an order that will most effectively lead worshipers into an experience of God through this biblical theme so that they might be changed?" We make it a point not to start the service the same way each week in order to avoid a feeling of predictability that can prevent people from truly opening themselves to the work of the Spirit in worship. I've found that when worship is too predictable, people unconsciously build up defenses that keep them from experiencing God. Surprise can open hearts and minds in wonderful ways. This approach generates a sense of anticipation as people wonder what is going to happen in worship that week. Each service becomes a unique event, not just a repetitious set of rituals. As one member confided to me, "I hate to go out of town over a Sunday because I don't want to miss what is going to happen in church!"

This doesn't mean we change things just for the sake of change. If every aspect of worship is new or different each week, people will never become familiar enough with the forms of our worship to enter into its content. Imagine if all the songs were new each week—no one would ever sing! If the most effective way to order something is the same as we did it last week, then we will do it that way. There are certain elements, such as the welcome and the sending, that consistently fit into a certain part of the service by virtue of their function, but we can still add variety through the way we do them. There are other elements, such as announcements and intercessory prayer, that we consistently include in the same place in the service because that is where they seem to work the best. Variety keeps the service fresh, but some familiarity will help people enter more fully into the worship experience.

We don't try to include all twelve of the previously listed elements every week, but we have identified some elements as weekly, some as biweekly, some as monthly, and some as occasional. Your own denominational tradition and missional focus will help you determine which elements need to be included more consistently and which can be done occasionally in your services. There are some forms of these elements that we use repeatedly so people become familiar with them (e.g., songs, creeds, the Lord's Prayer) and other forms that we create each week so they are fresh and relevant to our topic. The goal is to find a healthy balance between innovation and consistency.

An Order with Purpose

When we sit down to create a worship order, it is critical to understand the overall goal of the service: What kind of experience are we hoping to facilitate? Where are we trying to take the worshipers? How do we think we can help them allow the Spirit to move them in that direction? What do we hope will happen in their lives because of it? It is also critical that we analyze the specific purpose of each element: Why are we including this in the service? How will this element affect the worshipers? Does this add something significant, or will we be better off without it? How does this element fit into our overall purpose? How does it relate to the other elements in the service?

Once we have an understanding of the function of the elements, we can begin to experiment with different combinations that will lead people into an experience of God. This is a process of trial and error with allowance for creativity and modification. Our programming director puts together a rough draft of the worship order two weeks before the date of the service. In our weekly worship planning meetings, we discuss the order, brainstorm other approaches, and finalize it as a group during the week before the service.

There are some consistent principles we have learned that help guide our process:

Open strong: It is important to grab people's attention right off the bat by setting the tone for what is to come. If you start off with a low-energy element that is boring or confusing, you will lose some people right away. Try a film clip, an upbeat special-music piece, a high-energy set of worship songs, or something else that will draw people in even if they are distracted and disconnected. Sometimes we begin with a brief verbal welcome and newcomers' information but then transition quickly to a more engaging element.

Introduce the theme: We find that it is important to let people know something about the focus and direction of the service early on so they can understand what's happening and why. This does not mean giving away the whole message of the service up front. We try to tell them just enough near the beginning of the service to whet their appetites so they can connect more fully with the meaning of the elements.

Deliver the goods: Follow through with the substantive spiritual content that people are seeking. You don't want to lead people somewhere and then leave them hanging. It is easy to get so focused on developing creative elements that you never offer the actual biblical content that ultimately fuels the process of transformation. In Experiential Worship, ideally the entire service conveys the message, but this responsibility ultimately rests on the preacher.

Invite response: If we hope to move spiritual seekers into an authentic life of discipleship, it is critical that every worship experience gives people an opportunity to respond in some way to the message. This typically will come in the last third of the worship service.

Housekeeping items: In every service, there is certain information that needs to be conveyed for the sake of the newcomer or the community as a whole that does not relate directly to the theme of the service. We all know how this can seriously interrupt the flow of the service. Try connecting these non-thematic elements to elements that have more meaning. For instance, we often connect the information newcomers need to know with our theme introduction near the beginning of the service. Likewise, we usually do our program announcements during the offering and describe them as other ways we can offer our lives back to God.

Finish with hope: While there are notable exceptions (such as a reflective Good Friday service), we like to end the service on a positive, encouraging note. The use of a benediction, a motivational sending, and an upbeat closing song contributes to this, but it is also good to program other inspiring and empowering elements near the end of the service so that they act as a springboard for living out the message the other six days of the week.

WORSHIP THAT FLOWS

One of the keys to creating an effective Experiential Worship order is to see the service as a dynamic process through which you are going to lead people, not a static set of rituals ordered to fit some preconceived structure. We constantly ask, "What will people be experiencing at this moment in the worship gathering? How does this element fit with what comes before it? How does it lead into what follows?"

Sally Morgenthaler has led the way in teaching us how to design the movement of a worship gathering with her adjustable "hourglass" model for ordering a service, which gives attention to the beginning, middle, and end of a service.[1] We mentioned the importance of beginning strong and ending with hope. These are the ends of the hourglass. However, in the emerging postmodern culture, our task is becoming more complicated. As we move out of the linear models of modernity and incorporate creative elements, we can no longer simply progress from one end of the hourglass to the other. The path to experiencing God is a winding road. The road map we are creating is meant to help people navigate various twists and turns along the way but always with the same goal in mind: helping people find their way to an encounter with God.

Your job is like the weaver who has to pick the right strands and weave them in and out of the warp at the right places to create a meaningful pattern. An Experiential Worship order creates spiritual momentum that moves people into a deeper encounter with God. We call this momentum "flow." As you consider the various elements of a given service, ask the following questions: How can we connect these pieces in such a way that they will draw people into an experience of God? How can we grab their attention in the beginning? How can we help them set aside their distractions, lower their defenses, abandon their denials, and begin to open themselves to the Word and the Spirit? How can we help them not only listen to a message and understand it but then respond by applying it to their lives? How can we move people from the conviction of sin, to the joy of forgiveness, to the freedom of truth, to the power of the Spirit?

In our worship-planning meeting, we give attention not only to the order of the elements but also to the transitions between those elements. Transitions are the glue that holds the pieces together and allows momentum to build. You may have a song that follows the sermon beautifully, but if there is not an adequate transition from one to the other, the flow of experience may be lost. An effective transition can be as simple as a short sentence, a brief prayer, a meaningful gesture, a physical posture, a musical introduction, a change in lighting, a moment of silence, or nothing at all. But effective transitions do not happen automatically; they grow out of carefully considering how best to connect each element.

I love to preach in our Experiential Worship gatherings because often the spiritual flow is so strong by the time I start speaking that it carries through my message and makes my words far more effective. Likewise, some of the elements we do later in the service are very simple and might seem unimportant by themselves, but by the time we get there, even the simplest act can have profound spiritual impact because of the momentum that has been built up. We once did a series on the wisdom of Proverbs and concluded with a service focused on the importance of our elders. Toward the end of that service, the worshipers laid hands on those who were over seventy years old and spoke a blessing over them in unison. By itself, this blessing might have been a sentimental exercise in appreciation, but coming near the end of that service, the Holy Spirit made it a holy moment of healing and renewal. This is the power of worship that flows; this is the goal of an Experiential Worship order.

Chapter 24

STEP FIVE:
LEADING EXPERIENTIALLY

SHOW THEM THE WAY

Periodically, I lead groups on two-week experiential retreats to the Holy Land; we call these retreats "In the Footsteps of Jesus." These are not your typical tours through a tourist company but independent, off-the-beaten-path adventure pilgrimages. I will never forget the feeling I had as we boarded the plane the first time I led such a trip: absolute terror! Although I had spent lots of time in the places we were going, suddenly the reality hit me that I was totally responsible for safely leading these twenty people around the world.

Leading Experiential Worship is a little like that. We are called not only to be the mapmakers on this adventure but the spiritual guides as well. It is one thing to plan and prepare for an experiential service, but when the time comes for us to actually lead people into an encounter with God, it can be a little scary. It is important that we do not try to do it alone. All along, I have emphasized that one or even a few people cannot effectively implement Experiential Worship; it is always a team effort. The same is true of leading Experiential Worship: we cannot do it from an ivory tower; it can only be done as a team.

Preparing to lead as a team begins once the worship order has been finalized. As a group, we always work through the specifics of how the service will be led: who will lead each element, where it will happen, how we will transition into it, how we will transition to the next element, what the lighting requirements are, and so on. It is very easy for some of us to skip this step and decide it is easier to "wing it," saying things such as, "We'll just let the Spirit lead." The truth is, the Spirit can lead us ahead of time in a planning meeting and the outcome is usually far more effective. We absolutely must allow the Spirit to guide us throughout the entire process, including while we are actually leading the service. We do not want to become so programmed that we leave no room for the Spirit to work in the moment, but we also do not want to shirk our own responsibility to be as prepared as possible so we can more effectively follow the Spirit's leading in the moment. Good preparation gives you the freedom to be spontaneous in the Spirit without sacrificing effectiveness.

FLYING AS ONE

Have you ever watched a flock of birds swooping up and down wildly in the sky but by some miracle seeming to move as one? This is the kind of communication and coordination required to effectively lead Experiential Worship. If a single person is leading the entire service, all of the coordination can go on inside that person's head. However, once we decide to engage people's hearts, souls, minds, and bodies, flying solo becomes impossible. This means that all people and teams involved in leading the worship experience have to know not only what they are doing, when they are doing it, and how they are going to do it, but also what, when, and how the others are going to do *their* parts!

To coordinate all of this information, our team has developed a "Worship Order Chart" (see appendix C). This includes on one sheet of paper all of the information each person or team needs in order to lead their aspect of the worship experience. In our case, we list each worship element and then, in column form, record the following information: who is leading the element, what is happening on the screen, what is coming through the sound system, what is happening with the lights, and any logistical notes about the element. This way, all of the people involved know what they are supposed to be doing at any given point in the service. Because we are doing something significantly different each week, it is important for us to estimate the minutes each element will require and try to stay with the sixty- to seventy-minute window that our worship schedule and parking lot will allow. This lets us adjust as necessary if things are running significantly longer than expected. You will want to come up with a chart more or less complex than ours to match the scope of your needs and then allow it to evolve as you develop your Experiential Worship ministry.

A Dry Run

Almost every church has a weekly rehearsal for the musicians who lead the musical aspect of their worship. When we expand the creative aspects of worship to encompass all of the arts and try to bring them together into a powerful experience of God, it becomes necessary to have a weekly rehearsal of the service as a whole; we call this rehearsal our "worship run-through." This is not in order to create a slick, polished "show" but is to make sure everything is in place and works so that the spiritual flow of authentic worship is not interrupted by logistical issues. We do not necessarily run through every element of the service in its entirety, but we do perform a dry run on all the technical aspects of the service and make sure the transitions will work and flow well. Unforeseen bugs get worked out at the run-through, and those responsible for making sure everything comes together are more prepared to help create the flow.

It makes sense to connect this run-through to the primary weekly musical rehearsal because that typically involves the most people and usually is already established. We do our run-through at the end of the band and singers' rehearsal. Our music director and programming director coordinate their teams and make sure everyone is on the same page. The volunteers on the tech team are in the control booth preparing the visuals for the screens, adjusting the soundboard, programming the lighting board, and so on while the musicians are rehearsing the music. Then at the appropriate time, they all come together for a prayer of focus and go through all the music and other elements, practicing the transitions, graphics, lighting, and sound. The programming director decides which creative elements need to be done at the run-through and which can simply be a placeholder (for example, "Now the dance team will begin their dance at the center of the platform"). This approach may seem difficult to implement in your setting, but try experimenting until you find a way to rehearse how all the creative elements of your worship will fit together.

PERSONAL PREPARATION

It has often been said that you cannot lead others where you have not been or are not willing to go yourself, and this is especially true in Experiential Worship. The only reason I was able to lead that trip to the Holy Land effectively is because I had previously spent plenty of time there myself. It is not enough to talk about the idea of experiencing God. It is not enough to plan opportunities for others to encounter God. It is not enough to invite others to experience God in a service you have designed. You yourself must be a seeker of God and willing to lead the way by your own experience. First and foremost, this begins in your personal prayer and worship life.

As worship leaders, there is no substitute for daily drawing from the well of intimate time with God in prayer and worship. This means growing beyond perfunctory requests and rigid structures into a prayer life that is personal, intimate, and filled with adoration of the God we serve.[1] Worship is essentially a form of prayer, and it is in our private "prayer closet" that we best learn to worship God and lead others to that well of Living Water. Prayer paves the way to experiencing God.

When the time comes to lead an Experiential Worship gathering, it is essential that all those who are leading have one final opportunity to connect spiritually and logistically. The half hour before a service is always chaotic, with musicians warming up, worshipers arriving, and volunteers showing up late. In the midst of all this, our team has found that it is imperative to come together for final coordination and prayer. We gather in our prayer chapel about five minutes before the service starts and quickly go over the worship order to clarify or adjust any transitions. Then we join hands and one of our trained volunteer prayer ministers prays specifically for those leading and for those who have come to encounter God. These faithful servants then continue to pray for us and for the congregation as we go out to lead. What an encouragement to know that we are being lifted up in prayer throughout the service! Although we have multiple services, we gather like this before each service, making adjustments based on how things went in the previous service, and then we pray again.

INCARNATIONAL LEADERSHIP

All parents know that what we *do* has far greater effect on our kids than what we *say*. The same is true of leading Experiential Worship. We cannot *tell* people to experience God, but we can *show* them what it is like. To lead this kind of worship, you must be willing to enter into it yourself. The joy and life-changing power of authentic encounters with God are contagious: people will catch it from those who lead them. When they see someone sincerely seeking God and taking the risk of opening his or her heart, soul, mind, and body to God in worship, they will follow that example.

Experiential Worship leaders are willing to be real and somewhat transparent while they lead. It has often been said that we are to be not worship leaders but "lead worshipers." There is no room here for putting on a show or faking it. People are turned off by a slick performance and can smell a phony a mile off. And obviously, there are appropriate boundaries for public disclosure—this is not a form of group therapy or a time to air dirty laundry! But unless we genuinely seek to worship God with all that we are and are honest with those we lead, we cannot be able to effectively lead others into that experience. This applies to all who lead, not just those who are "up front," such as pastors and music leaders. The members of our tech team make it a point to engage in the worship experience as much as they can, even though they are busy with their tasks and are not front and center. Sometimes I will look up into the control booth and see the sound technicians closing their eyes or lifting their hands. We are worshipers *before* we are singers or guitar players or sound technicians or ushers or pastors.

BALANCING WORSHIP AND LEADERSHIP

Unfortunately, as lead worshipers, we do not have the luxury of losing ourselves in worship the way others do, because we have to keep the task of leadership in focus. Maybe you've had the experience of driving through a beautiful area while everyone in the car is oohing and aahing, but you can't fully appreciate the scenery because you have to keep your eyes on the road. This is the predicament of those who lead Experiential Worship. If the tech team has their eyes closed when they need to be watching what is happening, the flow of the service will be compromised. The challenge of leading worship by worshiping is learning to balance your personal experience with the experience of the congregation. This means engaging in worship as fully as possible while still remaining aware of what is coming and what your role is. This is not something that happens automatically, but it can be learned over time.

Experiential Worship leadership requires a simultaneous awareness of God, the flow of the service, and the people you are leading. We are constantly looking ahead to what is coming so that we are able to keep the momentum of the service flowing. We remain sensitive to the leading of the Holy Spirit so that we are ready for whatever adjustments or inspirations might come. Again, when you are well prepared, you are able to incorporate insight and opportunities as they arise, without sacrificing the overall quality of the service. At the same time, you watch what is happening with the people to see how they are reacting and to stay in tune with the experience they are having.

It is sometimes hard to anticipate how people are going to react to various elements in a service. Because I spend so much time working on these elements, I sometimes lose touch with the impact of what we are doing and then find myself surprised when people laugh or cry or respond in other intense ways. We need to read these reactions in the moment so we can adjust appropriately and proceed with sensitivity. The worship leader who is out of touch with the congregation and the Spirit can miss or even ruin those poignant holy moments that are so ripe for life-change.

It is also important to remember that while we model worship as we lead, the whole point of worship leadership is to direct people to God and not to ourselves. As David Arcos, director of creative arts at Mosaic, explained to me, "Worship leaders cannot be invisible, because their role is to embody worship for the people, but they must be transparent and point people to the One we worship."[2] Those who lead Experiential Worship must find that tricky balance of showing people how to worship without allowing themselves to become the focus of that worship. This requires genuine humility, a heart focused on God, and a sincere desire to lead others to his throne. The more we become lead worshipers who show others the way by offering our whole selves to God, the more others will follow our example with their own passionate offering.

Chapter 25

STEP SIX: EVALUATION

A LEARNING CULTURE

You've heard the old adage "Give someone a fish, feed them for a day; teach someone to fish, feed them for a lifetime." This can be expanded to say, "Equip someone to keep learning better ways to fish, feed a village for a lifetime." Those who plan and lead Experiential Worship will develop a learning culture so that they can continue to increase their effectiveness and remain relevant to a constantly changing culture.

As soon as we latch on to the "right" way of doing worship, we immediately become obsolete to a world that is always on the move. If we are not learning and growing in our effectiveness, we are losing ground. I try to teach my sons to see every experience in their lives, good and bad, as an opportunity to learn. In the same way, every worship gathering is an experiment in the laboratory of ministry. This means investing time in regular evaluation.

Our worship planning team meets every Tuesday, and we begin by evaluating the previous Sunday. We each say what we think went well and why. Then we point out areas that did not work as we had hoped and discuss ideas of how they might have worked better. Nothing is exempt from this evaluation (including the pastor's message!), but we try not to personalize the criticism. Feedback requires trust and maturity, and when offered with liberal affirmation, it can help build both. When there is necessary feedback that would be difficult for an individual to receive in a group setting, I make it a point to offer it one-on-one with a person prior to the meeting or I make general references to the issue without singling that person out.

It is important to maintain balance in the evaluation process. Most of us tend to remember one critical comment and forget a hundred affirmations. If worship evaluation is leaving the team feeling discouraged, the balance needs to be tipped toward reinforcing the positive, showing sensitivity, and speaking the truth in love. If members of the team are not secure enough to receive constructive feedback, they will need to grow in confidence and maturity so they can learn from such input and grow in their effectiveness. Experiential Worship is about changing people's lives. There is no room for comfortable mediocrity or defensive stagnancy—there is too much at stake!

A WORTHWHILE SACRIFICE

For many of us, regular evaluation might seem like a good ideal, but in the back of our minds, we are thinking that there simply is not time for this final step. Deeper down inside, there is a part of us that really doesn't want to face the accountability of such a process. But we dare not give in to the temptation to skip this critical final step! Regular evaluation is what moves us from simply trying to implement a static model to developing a constantly evolving, continually improving process. If we want to catch only one fish a day, then we should keep doing it the same way we were taught. But what happens when the fish population changes and our method no longer works? Only through a process of intentional evaluation will we grow in our effectiveness and be able to adapt to the ever-changing culture.

Recently, a former member of our pastoral staff worshiped with us on a Sunday morning. Three years earlier, she had participated in planning and leading our early experiential services and had been a part of our weekly evaluation times. After the service, this pastor raved about how powerful and meaningful the worship experience was. Her comments made me realize just how far we had come in three years. She said, "I guess all those evaluation meetings were worth it after all!" To invest time in honest and constructive evaluation is a personal risk and sacrifice, but it is well worth the cost. It is the only way we will be able to continue to catch fish—and who knows, maybe eventually we will be able to feed the whole village!

TAKING THE FIRST STEP

Maybe you have finished reading this section and still feel like Experiential Worship is an unattainable goal for you and your church. Perhaps you look at the demographics of who is sitting in your pews and think, *This might work for an urban church plant targeted at postmodern GenXers, but it will never work here!* My church is comprised of a tremendous mix of ages, family situations, and backgrounds. We are an established congregation of a mainline denomination, and I am constantly amazed at the variety of people who love to experience God more fully in worship gatherings that engage the heart, soul, mind, and body. Generational differences are significant, but in the emerging postmodern culture, there is a growing hunger for intergenerational community. Our teenagers are glad they can enjoy the primary worship gathering of our church rather than having to be exiled to an "age-appropriate" service. One Sunday I was approached after worship by two newcomers. They both expressed how powerful and moving the experience had been for them. Amazingly, they were more than eighty years apart in age!

Maybe you are thinking that the traditional style of worship in your church simply won't work for Experiential Worship. Each Sunday, our church has two services very contemporary in style, and we also have a traditional, liturgical service. Believe it or not, even our traditional service incorporates the principles described in this book. We use our heritage of ancient liturgy and classic hymns but arrange them to lead people into an encounter with God, incorporating the creative use of video, drama, poetry, graphics, and so on. No matter what your style of worship, you can make it more experiential in nature if you are willing to implement the principles of Experiential Worship.

Maybe you are thinking your congregation is just too small to do something like this, but mine is not a huge megachurch with unlimited resources.[1] Your church may be smaller or larger, but every ministry is a product of the gifts God has given the members of that community. If you are willing to cast a vision and unleash the gifts of your church, the Spirit of God will help you implement Experiential Worship in a unique way that reflects your congregation.

Maybe you feel that the politics of your church would make it impossible to move toward more experiential gatherings. Implementing Experiential Worship sparked serious conflict and forced us to face dysfunction in our church, but we came to see this was exactly what we needed to spark healthy growth and renewal. The question is whether your leaders understand the biblical vision of providing life-changing encounters with God and are willing to lead in that direction.

Whatever your resistance to implementing Experiential Worship, I understand. It is risky and difficult to venture out of our comfort zones. But remember that every worthwhile journey begins with the first step. Don't look at the whole map at once; just look at the first leg of the journey. Start with the first step: planning the preaching and worship themes further ahead of time. Then begin to distribute those themes to everyone who is interested in and gifted for creative worship planning. Then pick a time to meet just for the sharing of ideas. Don't set a strict timetable or establish rigid criteria for what must be accomplished. Offer it to God in prayer, share the vision of Experiential Worship with your leaders and teammates, and start the journey with some concrete steps. Before you know it, the wind of the Spirit will have filled your sails and you will be heading for uncharted territory on the most exciting adventure imaginable!

Conclusion

FURTHER UP AND FURTHER IN

*Beloved, we are God's children now; what we will be has not yet
been revealed. What we do know is this: when he is revealed,
we will be like him, for we will see him as he is.*

1 JOHN 3:2

We began this journey together with stories of the four historical streams of worship. What are the stories that constitute the fabric of your ministry? When I close my eyes, an endless parade of faces from our congregation marches through my mind: Jerry, Ellen, Brad, Wendy, Phil, Carol, Jim, Libona, Howie, Laverne, Brian—and on and on it goes, like a triumphal victory procession, giving glory to God. Each one is a precious child of God, a living example of Jesus' transforming grace, touched and changed by regularly encountering God in worship. They are a reminder to me of why I do this. They are an encouragement to me when I am tired and discouraged. They are the living testimony that planning and leading Experiential Worship is worth whatever sacrifice it takes.

There are many endeavors I have undertaken in my life that, if I had known ahead of time all that they would entail, I probably would not have had the courage to begin or the determination to continue. Yet as I look back on my life, I can see that these are precisely the most important experiences of my life, the things that have produced whatever image of Christ has been formed in me. If we knew ahead of time the personal cost involved, books would not be written, frontiers would not be explored, marriage vows would not be exchanged, children would not be born, congregations would not be planted, and churches would not be reformed. What a loss it would be if we allowed their steep price to keep us from pursuing the most important things in history and in life!

Jesus recognized the high cost of his calling, and though he would have liked to let that cup pass, he did not. Instead, he prayed to his heavenly Father, "Not my will, but yours be done" (Luke 22:42). Jesus did not try to hide this steep cost from his followers but invited them to "deny themselves and take up their cross and follow me. For those who want to save their life will lose it, and those who lose their life for my sake will find it" (Matthew 16:24-25).

In the postmodern parable/film *The Matrix*, Morpheus presents Neo with an excruciating choice: take the red pill and return to a life of comfortable delusion or take the blue pill and discover the challenging truth of the world as it really is. I don't want to be less than fully honest with you. To take the blue pill, to dislodge our heads from comfortable sand and face the reality that the world is radically changing, is costly. To engage this emerging culture with worship that is both biblically faithful and culturally authentic is costly. To bring together the historical streams of biblical worship in experiences that invite people to encounter God with their heart, soul, mind, and strength is costly. If you answer this call, you will face criticism, opposition, conflict, division, and rejection. You will endure times of doubt, discouragement, and disappointment. It was that early postmodern martyr Dietrich Bonhoeffer who, after describing the costly nature of God's freely given grace, said, "What has cost God much cannot be cheap for us."[1] Yet, as he himself discovered so dramatically, it is precisely in this loss of life for Jesus' sake that we are resurrected!

In his classic allegorical adventure *The Chronicles of Narnia*, C. S. Lewis takes us on an adventure through a magical wardrobe and into the land of Narnia with Peter, Susan, Edmund, and Lucy. They face untold dangers, fear, uncertainty, and sacrifices. But through all of this, they come to know Aslan, the great Lion from across the Sea, and discover so much more of who they were meant to be. This journey through Narnia was the greatest experience of their lives. When things were most difficult, when the group was tempted to turn back and retreat to more familiar territory, Aslan would remind them that they were only on the edge of this adventure and there was still so much to discover. To express their faith in that promise and their determination to follow Aslan, their cry became, "Further up and further in! Further up and further in!"[2]

We are on the edge of an adventure called Experiential Worship. The world has radically changed around us and the question is, will we take the blue pill, lift our heads from the sand, and step through the wardrobe into this unknown land? God is calling us to lead people further up and further in to the transforming wonder of holistic encounters with him. Recovering the biblical paradigm for Experiential Worship is one of the keys that will enable us to lead people to the "other side" of this historic time of cultural change.

To answer this call will cost us everything. If we are willing to pay that price by loving God with all our heart, soul, mind, and strength and helping others do the same, we will discover this priceless grace is worth infinitely more than it costs. The author of Hebrews describes how Jesus discovered this truth: "Jesus the pioneer and perfecter of our faith, who for the sake of the joy that was set before him endured the cross, disregarding its shame, and has taken his seat at the right hand of the throne of God" (Hebrews 12:2). Learning about and leading others into Experiential Worship is a journey into the kingdom of God that ultimately will never end. It is a glorious foretaste of the eternal feast that has already begun. Jesus, our Pioneer and Perfecter, is the one calling us to take up our cross and follow him. Can you hear him calling? "Further up and further in. Further up and further in. *Further up and further in!*"

Appendix A

WORSHIP THEMES

This is an example of a worship theme that was the first of a seven-week spiritual growth series based on John 15 called "Secrets of a Fruit-Full Life." This document was sent out to the members of the creative arts team prior to a brainstorming session:

WORSHIP THEME FOR MAY 16

Theme: God is the source of all spiritual fruitfulness. Our role is choosing to stay connected through obedience and disciplines.

Scripture: John 15:1-11: *I am the vine, you are the branches. Those who abide in me and I in them bear much fruit.*

Synopsis: *Secrets of a Fruit-Full Life: "Clinging to the Vine"* We all know that our lives are meant for more than they are now. No matter where we are, we all sense there is so much more to discover, so much more to become. We want our lives to matter, to produce fruit that will be a blessing to others, bring glory to God, and fulfill our sense of purpose. We try again and again, but it doesn't seem to work. While we may accomplish certain goals and produce certain results, there are things about ourselves that we just can't seem to change, no matter how hard we try. There are things we simply can't produce no matter what we do. On the last night he was with his disciples, Jesus revealed secrets of spiritual growth and fruitfulness that would revolutionize our lives if we would discover and embrace them. He told us that we are like branches on a grapevine, created to grow and produce a vintage harvest. The secret of the fruitful branch lies in its relationship to the vine, which is the source of its growth and productivity. Jesus said that as we learn to abide in him, he will produce the fruitful growth in us that we cannot produce in ourselves. The growth and the fruit comes from God; no amount of effort on our part could accomplish it. Our job is to abide, to remain connected to him, so that the growth can flow through him into us. Fruit will naturally begin to appear. This is the secret of the fruitful life: not trying harder to be different, but learning how to abide in Jesus so that he can grow us and produce eternal fruit through us!

Content Ideas: 1 Corinthians 3:6-7; Philippians 2:12-13; Galatians 5:16-26; 1 John 3:2; Ephesians 4:15

Music Ideas:

Creative Theme Ideas:
- Heart (Volitional):
- Mind (Intellectual):
- Soul (Emotional):
- Body (Physical):

Appendix B

CREATIVE THEMES

This is the updated version of the "Worship Themes" document that was sent out to all of the creative teams for implementation after the planning team determined which ideas to use from the creative arts team's brainstorming session. It included specific instructions, deadlines, and other details for each team.

CREATIVE ELEMENTS FOR MAY 16

Theme: God is the source of all spiritual fruitfulness. Our role is choosing to stay connected through obedience and disciplines.

Scripture: John 15:1-11: *I am the vine, you are the branches. Those who abide in me and I in them bear much fruit.*

Title: *Secrets of a Fruit-Full Life: "Clinging to the Vine"*

Content Ideas: 1 Corinthians 3:6-7; Philippians 2:12-13; Galatians 5:16-26; 1 John 3:2; Ephesians 4:15

Music Ideas: Special music: "Empty Me," by Jeremy Camp; include prayer of confession during song in opening worship set, followed by affirmation of forgiveness

Creative Theme Ideas:

- Heart (Volitional): On two walls, hang butcher-paper murals of a vine; following Communion, invite people to draw a branch on the vine and sign it as a symbol of their decision to become/stay connected to Jesus through faith and disciplines

- Mind (Intellectual): Use clip from *The Gospel of John* film (The Visual Bible) to present the Scripture reading from John 15:1-11; use projected diagrams of the vine and the branches to illustrate the processes of "transpiration" and "translocation," which cause vines to grow branches and produce fruit; quote from Henry Cloud and John Townsend's book *How People Grow*, and offer it for sale after service

- Soul (Emotional): Evoke a vineyard feeling on the platform by building trellises under the screens and creating twisted paper grapevines with branches, leaves, and grapes; use clips from the film *A Walk in the Clouds* to illustrate life on a vineyard, especially "the root of our lives" scene and "the joyful harvest" scene; use "The Vine and Branches" poem from the Holy Joe's website during worship; ask a member to give a four-minute testimony explaining how he or she has learned that a daily quiet time helps him or her "abide" in Jesus more consistently and deeply

- Body (Physical): Connect Communion to the message by emphasizing eating bread and drinking wine as ways to "abide" in Jesus

Appendix C

WORSHIP ORDER

$\mathcal{T}$he chart on the following page outlines the order of worship designed by the planning team and shows each person or team how their part fits with all the others.

Order of Worship for May 16

Time		Element	People/Teams	Graphics	Lighting	Audio	Logistics
9:20	10:50	**Prayer**	All Teams	Announcements Prequel	(Welcome) \n\n Shades Up	Worship CD	Sound checks, platform normal
9:30	11:00	**Welcome** \n **Theme Intro**	Pastor Bob	Welcome Slide	(Welcome) \n\n Shades Down	Bob's lapel mic	Explain new series
9:32	11:02	**Singing Together** \n "Resonate" \n "Open the Eyes of My Heart" \n Confession/Forgiveness \n (Lea pray/sit)	Lea/Worship Team	Lyric Slides with Video Backgrounds	(Singing)	Lea/Band/Vocals	Lea leads confession during "Open the Eyes" Finish with affirmation of forgiveness
9:42	11:12	**Message Intro**	Pastor Bob	Sermon Slides	(Preaching)	Bob's lapel mic	
9:47	11:17	**Film Clip** \n *The Gospel of John*	Tech Team	DVD 1.5 (24:00–25:49)	(Video)	Video	Use subtitles
9:49	11:19	**Message, Part 1** \n "Clinging to the Vine" \n John 15:1-11	Pastor Bob	Sermon Slides	(Preaching)	Bob's lapel mic	
10:01	11:31	**Testimony**	Cindi W.	Testimony Slide	(Preaching)	Cindi's mic	From center
10:05	11:35	**Message, Part 2**	Pastor Bob	Sermon Slides	(Preaching)	Bob's lapel mic	
10:10	11:40	**Poem** \n "The Vine and Branches"	Tech Team	Poem Slide	(Video)	CD	Off platform, prerecorded
10:12	11:42	**Film Clip** \n *A Walk in the Clouds*	Tech Team	DVD 1.9 (45:06–46:43)	(Video)	Video	Use subtitles
10:14	11:44	**Message Conclusion**	Pastor Bob	Sermon Slides	(Preaching)	Bob's lapel mic	
10:16	11:46	**Film Clip** \n *A Walk in the Clouds*	Tech Team	DVD 1.10 (53:03–54:23)	(Video)	Video	No subtitles
10:18	11:48	**Special Music** \n "Empty Me"	Lea/Band	Special Music Slide	(Band)	Lea/Band/Vocals	Tie in with thematic intro
10:22	11:52	**Profession of Faith**	Pastor Bob	Vine Creed		Bob's lapel mic	Standing
10:24	11:54	**Communion** \n Words of Institution \n Lord's Prayer \n Vine/Branches Instructions \n "I'm in Need of You" \n "Needful Hands" \n "Hallelujah"	Pastor Greg \n Lea/Worship Team \n Lea	Communion Slide \n Lyric Slides	(Singing)	Pastors Bob/Greg \n Lea/Band/Vocals	Kneeling Communion Invite people to draw on vine after receiving Communion
10:34	12:04	**Community Prayer**	Pastor Greg	Prayer Slide	(Prayer) \n Shades Up	Greg's lapel mic	Standing
10:36	12:06	**Time of Giving** \n **Announcements**	Pastor Greg	Announcement Slides	(Announcement)	Greg's lapel mic	
10:38	12:08	**Blessing and Sending** \n "Your Great Name We Praise"	Pastors Bob/Greg \n Lea/Worship Team	Lyric Slides	(Announcement) \n (Closing)	Greg \n Lea/Worship Team	Standing

Appendix D

FRACTAL TEAMS

This is one example of how we have structured our teams for planning and implementing Experiential Worship.

Appendix E

Web-Based Resources

*E*xplore these websites to find resources for planning, implementing, and leading Experiential Worship.

www.experientialworship.com	Experiential Worship leaders sharing ideas and resources
www.sacramentis.com	Sally Morgenthaler's comprehensive resource for worship
www.ancientfutureworship.com	Robert Webber's resources for worship planning
www.vintagefaith.com	A look into Dan Kimball's emerging church
www.theooze.com	Perspectives on postmodern Christianity
www.emergentvillage.org	A conversation of the "emerging church"
www.greenbelt.org.uk	A European perspective on emerging Christianity and the arts
www.268generation.com	Cutting-edge worship music
www.soulsurvivor.com	Cutting-edge worship music
www.worshiptogether.com	Cutting-edge worship music
www.heartofworship.com	Cutting-edge worship music
www.ionabooks.com	Ancient rituals and liturgy for contemporary worship
www.taize.fr	Resources for contemplative worship
www.hollywoodjesus.com	Relating film to biblical faith
www.dramashare.org	Free drama scripts
www.worshipdance.org	Using dance in worship
www.preachingtoday.com	Searchable database for stories and illustrations

www.eyeeffects.com	visual images for worship
www.radiatefilms.com	Still and video backgrounds for worship
www.worshipfilms.com	Devotional video for worship
www.highwayvideo.com	Creative video for worship
www.royaltyfreeart.com	Fine-art images for free
www.gettyimages.com	Quality stock photography
www.artbeats.com	Exceptional stock video footage
www.extraordinaryimages.net	Stock video footage of people, the world, and nature
www.shopping.discovery.com	Documentary footage
www.fowlerinc.com	Discount supplier for worship-related technology products

Notes

Introduction

1. Louie Giglio, *The Air I Breathe: Worship As a Way of Life* (Sisters, Ore.: Multnomah, 2003), p. 73.

Chapter 1

1. Matt Redman, "Revelation and Response," *The Heart of Worship Files* (Ventura, Calif.: Regal, 2003), p. 13.
2. Rick Warren, *The Purpose-Driven Life: What on Earth Am I Here For?* (Grand Rapids, Mich.: Zondervan, 2003), p. 109.
3. Sally Morgenthaler, "The One Thing . . ." *The Heart of Worship Files* (Ventura, Calif.: Regal, 2003), p. 31.
4. "The Westminster Confession of Faith," *The Book of Confessions* (New York: Office of the General Assembly of the Presbyterian Church [USA], 1999), p. 173.

Chapter 2

1. For example, note how Dallas Willard uses the term *soul* to describe a combination of "The Six Human Dimensions" in *Renovation of the Heart: Putting On the Character of Christ* (Colorado Springs, Colo.: NavPress, 2002), pp. 32-39.
2. For a photo of this graffiti, visit http://faculty.maxwell.syr.edu/gaddis/HST310/Sept11/Default.htm.

Chapter 3

1. Saint Augustine of Hippo, *Confessions*, X, 27 (New York: Penguin Books, 1961, 1985), p. 231.

2. Richard Foster, *Streams of Living Water: Celebrating the Great Traditions of Christian Faith* (New York: HarperCollins, 1999), p. xv.

3. See Dan Kimball, *Emerging Worship: Creating Worship Gatherings for New Generations* (Grand Rapids, Mich.: Zondervan, 2004) and *The Emerging Church* (Grand Rapids, Mich.: Zondervan, 2003).

4. Robert Webber, *The Younger Evangelicals: Facing the Challenges of the New World* (Grand Rapids, Mich.: Baker, 2003), p. 18. See also his *Ancient-Future Faith: Rethinking Evangelicalism for a Postmodern World* (Grand Rapids, Mich.: Baker, 1999).

5. Richard Foster, *Celebration of Discipline: The Path to Spiritual Growth* (New York: HarperCollins, 1978, 1988, 1998), p. 158.

6. Brian McLaren, *The Church on the Other Side* (Grand Rapids, Mich.: Zondervan, 2000).

7. George Barna, "Worship in the Third Millenium," in *Experiencing God in Worship* (Loveland, Colo.: Group, 2000), p. 14.

8. Leonard Sweet, *Post-Modern Pilgrims: First Century Passion for the 21st Century World* (Nashville: Broadman and Holman, 2000), pp. 29, 31, 33.

CHAPTER 4

1. C. S. Lewis, *Out of the Silent Planet* (New York: Macmillan, 1965), p. 95.

2. C. S. Lewis, *The Great Divorce* (New York: Macmillan, 1946), pp. 28-29.

3. Dallas Willard, *Renovation of the Heart* (Colorado Springs, Colo.: NavPress, 2002), p. 159.

4. Emphasis added to all Scripture verses in this paragraph.

5. Matt Redman, *The Unquenchable Worshipper: Coming Back to the Heart of Worship* (Ventura, Calif.: Regal, 2001), p. 41.

6. Lisa Tawn Bergren, *God Encounter: Experiencing the Power of Creative Prayer* (Colorado Springs, Colo.: Waterbrook, 2002), p. 2.

CHAPTER 5

1. Erwin McManus, *An Unstoppable Force: Daring to Become the Church God Had in Mind* (Loveland, Colo.: Group, 2001), pp. 132-145.

2. Leonard Sweet, *Post-Modern Pilgrims: First Century Passion for the 21st Century World* (Nashville: Broadman and Holman, 2000), p. 91.

CHAPTER 6

1. For more information on labyrinths, visit http://users.eastlink.ca/~standrewsunited/labyrin.htm. To find a labyrinth near you, go to wwll.veriditas.labyrinthsociety.org/.
2. Visit www.grouppublishing.com/prayerpath/kit.htm for more information.
3. Taken from the *Prayer Path Journal*, Lutheran Church of the Good Shepherd, Torrance, California.
4. Visit www.bergrendesign.com to see examples of this.
5. Dan Kimball, *Emerging Worship: Creating Worship Gatherings for New Generations* (Grand Rapids, Mich.: Zondervan, 2004), p. 34.

CHAPTER 9

1. I borrowed this phrase from a Bible study taught by John Ortberg at the 2001 National Pastors' Convention.
2. Ken Gire, *Windows of the Soul* (Grand Rapids, Mich.: Zondervan, 1996), p. 76.
3. Arthur Gordon, as quoted in Gire, p. 75.

CHAPTER 10

1. Visit www.dayspring.com/movies and click on the "Forgiven" icon to watch a presentation based on this painting.
2. Visit www.gospelofjohnthefilm.com.
3. Check out sites such as www.highwayvideo.com, http://lorray.spreadtheword.com, www.harbingeronline.com, www.angelhousemedia.com, www.midnightoilproductions.net, www.artbeats.com, and www.billabongfilms.com.
4. Scotty Smith, as described at the seminar "The Worship of Worship or the Worship of God," National Pastors' Convention, March 12, 2004.
5. Robert Webber, *Ancient-Future Faith: Rethinking Evangelism for a Postmodern World* (Grand Rapids, Mich.: Baker, 1999), p. 7.
6. See the work of Timothy J. Bergren at www.bergrendesign.com.

Chapter 14

1. Ken Gire, *Windows of the Soul* (Grand Rapids, Mich.: Zondervan, 1996), pp. 16-17.
2. Abraham Heschel, as quoted in Gire, p. 84.
3. Alexandr Solzhenitsyn, as quoted in Gire, p. 83.
4. Visit Mosaic church at www.mosaic.org.
5. David Arcos (church director of creative arts), in discussion with the author, June 2003.
6. Martin Luther, "Letter to Louis Senfl," *Luther's Works*, CD-ROM edition (Minneapolis: Fortress, 2001), vol. 49, p. 427.
7. Madeleine L'Engle, *Walking on Water: Reflections on Faith and Art* (Colorado Springs, Colo.: Waterbrook, 1980, 2001), pp. 83-84.
8. Sally Morgenthaler (worship innovator and author), in discussion with the author, July 2003.
9. Morgenthaler.
10. It is important to obtain copyright permission for all media you utilize. This can be done easily and affordably through organizations such as Christian Video Licensing International (www.cvli.org).

Chapter 15

1. Dietrich Bonhoeffer, *The Cost of Discipleship* (New York: Macmillan, 1937, 1963), p. 47.
2. Louie Giglio, *The Air I Breathe: Worship As a Way of Life* (Sisters, Ore.: Multnomah, 2003), p. 51.
3. Richard Foster, *Celebration of Discipline* (New York: HarperCollins, 1978, 1988, 1998), p. 7.
4. Foster, p. 158.

Chapter 16

1. For more information, visit www.purposedriven.com.
2. Max Lucado, *He Chose the Nails* (Nashville: Word, 2000).
3. Max Lucado, *He Did This Just for You* (Nashville: Word, 2001), pp. 9-29.

CHAPTER 17

1. Denny and Leesa Bellesi, *The Kingdom Assignment* (Grand Rapids, Mich.: Zondervan, 2001).

CHAPTER 18

1. For a description of the church as "cultural architects," see Erwin McManus, *An Unstoppable Force: Daring to Become the Church God Had in Mind* (Loveland, Colo.: Group, 2001), pp. 101-111.
2. H. Richard Niebuhr, *Christ and Culture* (New York: Harper and Row, 1951).
3. Brian McLaren, *The Church on the Other Side* (Grand Rapids, Mich.: Zondervan, 2000), p. 12.
4. Eddie Gibbs, *ChurchNext: Quantum Changes in How We Do Ministry* (Downers Grove, Ill.: InterVarsity, 2000), p. 11.
5. Sally Morgenthaler, *Worship Evangelism* (Grand Rapids, Mich.: Zondervan, 1995), pp. 80-86.

CHAPTER 22

1. An excellent practical resource for this from a European perspective is *Alternative Worship: Resources from and for the Emerging Church*, by Jonny Baker and Doug Gay (Grand Rapids, Mich.: Baker, 2003).
2. Wayne Cordeiro, *Doing Church as a Team* (Ventura, Calif.: Regal, 2001).

CHAPTER 23

1. Sally Morgenthaler, *Worship Evangelism* (Grand Rapids, Mich.: Zondervan, 1995), p. 163.

CHAPTER 24

1. See Rory Noland, *The Heart of the Artist: A Character-Building Guide for You and Your Ministry Team* (Grand Rapids, Mich.: Zondervan, 1999).
2. David Arcos (church director of creative arts), in discussion with the author, June 2003.

CHAPTER 25

1. At the time of this writing, our average weekly worship attendance is less than 450.

CONCLUSION

1. Dietrich Bonhoeffer, *The Cost of Discipleship* (New York: Macmillan, 1937, 1963), p. 48.
2. C. S. Lewis, *The Last Battle* (New York: Collier, 1956), p. 171.

About the Author

Bob Rognlien desires first and foremost to be a wholehearted worshiper of Jesus Christ. His greatest passion is to see people's lives changed through more complete biblical experiences of God in worship. Having lived on both coasts of the United States—as well as in Europe, the Middle East, and the Far East—Bob has worshiped God in many different cultures and traditions. A graduate of Princeton Theological Seminary, Bob has also studied in Tacoma, Washington; Berkeley, California; Kent, England; Berlin, Germany; and Jerusalem. He has served churches in New Jersey and Jerusalem as well as northern and southern California. As senior pastor of Lutheran Church of the Good Shepherd, he is privileged to be part of a life-changing community that is exploring new ways to worship God with heart, soul, mind, and strength. His greatest joy is sharing life with his wife, Pam, and his sons, Bobby and Luke. He makes his home with them in Torrance, California, where he loves to surf, ski, sail, paddle, backpack, cook, read, and go to the movies. Join the collaborative community of experiential worshipers at www.experientialworship.com or write to Bob at bob@experientialworship .com.

DEEPEN AND CONTINUE YOUR WORSHIP EXPERIENCE.

Buck-Naked Faith

Eric Sandras gives us an honest and encouraging challenge to dress our lives in a real friendship with God and nothing else.

Eric Sandras

ISBN-10: 1-57683-525-1
ISBN-13: 978-1-57683-525-8

Reclaiming God's Original Intent for the Church

By getting back to core values and away from energy-sapping obsessions, pastors learn how the focused, agile small church is the past—and the future—of the church.

**Wes Roberts and
Glenn Marshall**

ISBN-10: 1-57683-407-7
ISBN-13: 978-1-57683-407-7

Praise Habit

David Crowder redefines your perspective of a God beyond imagination and helps you develop a habit of praising Him by reflecting on targeted psalms from *The Message Remix*.

David Crowder

ISBN10: 1-57683-670-3
ISBN-13: 978-1-57683-670-5

To order copies, visit your local Christian bookstore,
call NavPress at 1-800-366-7788, or log on to www.navpress.com.
To locate a Christian bookstore near you,
call 1-800-991-7747.